Social Skills Activities For Secondary Students with Special Needs

Third Edition

Darlene Mannix

JB JOSSEY-BASS™
A Wiley Brand

Published by Jossey-Bass
A Wiley Imprint
John Wiley & Sons, Inc., 111 River Street, Hoboken, NJ 07030, USA

Jossey-Bass books and products are available through most bookstores. To contact Jossey-Bass directly call our Customer Care Department within the U.S. at 800-956-7739, outside the U.S. at 317-572-3986, or fax 317-572-4002.

Jossey-Bass also publishes its books in a variety of electronic formats. Some content that appears in print may not be available in electronic books.

Library of Congress Cataloging-in-Publication Data

Names: Mannix, Darlene, author.
Title: Social skills activities for secondary students with special needs / Darlene Mannix.
Description: Third Edition. | San Francisco : Jossey-Bass, [2022] | Series: Jossey-Bass Teacher | Originally published: West Nyack, N.Y. : Center for Applied Research in Education, c1998.
Identifiers: LCCN 2021051558 (print) | LCCN 2021051559 (ebook) | ISBN 9781119827429 (Paperback) | ISBN 9781119827481 (Adobe PDF) | ISBN 9781119827474 (ePub)
Subjects: LCSH: Developmentally disabled children—United States—Life skills guides. | Developmentally disabled children—Education (Secondary)—United States. | Life skills—Study and teaching (Secondary)—United States. | Social skills—Study and teaching (Secondary)—United States.
Classification: LCC HV894 .M365 2022 (print) | LCC HV894 (ebook) | DDC 305.9/085083—dc23/eng/20211209
LC record available at https://lccn.loc.gov/2021051558
LC ebook record available at https://lccn.loc.gov/2021051559

Cover Design: Wiley
Cover Images: © mhatzapa/Shutterstock, © Ola_view/Shutterstock, © Polina Tomtosova, © AnastasiaNi/Shutterstock
Printed and bound by CPI Group (UK) Ltd, Croydon, CR0 4YY

C9781119827429_230125

The manufacturer's authorized representative according to the EU General Product Safety Regulation is Wiley-VCH GmbH, Boschstr. 12, 69469 Weinheim, Germany, e-mail: Product_Safety@wiley.com.

About This Book

Social Skills Activities For Secondary Students with Special Needs, Third Edition, is a collection of lessons and activities designed to help secondary students with exceptionalities learn to improve their relationships with others.

The material in this book is designed to appeal to special needs students in several ways. The skills are presented in small, sequential steps. The topics are very specific and relevant. The lessons are designed for intentional, rather than incidental, learning. And although the topics covered are serious and important, humor and fun are always included whenever possible.

About the Author

Darlene Mannix has worked as an educator for more than thirty years and has taught a wide range of children, including students with learning disabilities, emotional disturbance, language disorders, reading disorders, and multiple disabilities. Mannix received her bachelor of science degree from Taylor University and her master's degree in learning disabilities from Indiana University. A past presenter at numerous educational conferences, including the Council for Exceptional Children, she is the author of many books, including the third edition of *Life Skills Activities for Secondary Students with Special Needs* (Jossey-Bass, 2021), *Life Skills Activities for Special Children* (Jossey-Bass, 2009), *Social Skills Activities for Special Children* (Jossey-Bass, 2008), and *Writing Skills Activities for Special Children* (Jossey-Bass, 2004). She has most recently worked as a Title 1 Reading Teacher.

This book is dedicated to Kara Mannix
"Such fun!"

Contents

Preface

Social Skills Activities for Secondary Students with Special Needs, Third Edition, was designed primarily for teachers working in a classroom setting, although parents, counselors, and anyone else working or living with secondary school–age children or teens in need of social skills training will also find it useful.

Social skills training is somewhat unique in that special needs students often require precise, intentional instruction for situations that are navigated easily and naturally by most students. Many special needs students have a hard time recognizing social cues from their environment, and they do not understand how to respond appropriately to people or events. Making and keeping friends is another area that is particularly challenging for special needs students.

The focus of this book is to present specific social skills for examination, training, and practice. The skills covered are based on the tasks and situations most commonly found in a secondary student's environment.

How This Book Is Organized

This book is organized into three main parts:

- Part One, "Personality Traits: What Are You Like?," seeks to help students answer questions about their basic personality traits. Using common examples, situations, and questions, students are guided into rating themselves on numerous traits using a spectrum with two views of one behavior at each end. Are they introverted? Are they extroverted? Group enthusiasts? Prefer to work alone? There are no right or wrong answers here; this is simply a way to help the students think about their personality traits. These traits will affect the students' successful navigation into social situations.
- Part Two, "Learning Basic Social Skills," delves right into specific skills that are helpful and necessary for an individual to acquire in order to be socially successful. This part of the book covers skills that relate to making a good impression (for instance, displaying acceptable behavior, listening, and communicating), skills for self-improvement (viewing situations realistically, controlling emotions, using a sense of humor appropriately, and so on), and skills for being around others (for example, respecting authority, being flexible, and negotiating).

  Each social skill unit contains instructor pages that give a brief rationale for teaching the skill, information on the worksheets within each unit (including suggested or typical answers for each worksheet), open-ended questions for deeper thinking and discussions, and numerous worksheets designed to teach the given social skill. Helpful websites are also listed for many of the skills.
- In Part Three, "Applying Social Skills in Life Situations," students are given the opportunity to apply the skills they learned in Part Two to a variety of situations at home, school, or work, among peers, within the community, and in leisure activities. Reference is often made to the social skills studied in Part Two to apply to practical examples in various settings.

How to Use These Materials

This book can serve as a general resource, with which you can address specific skills according to the needs of the student. You can also use the skills as the basis of an ongoing curriculum for daily social skills training within a classroom. The skill units can be used in any order.

Some ideas for implementing a social skills unit include the following:

- Introduce a weekly social skill that will be highlighted in your classroom and applied whenever possible to daily activities. Look for opportunities to mention the skill and point out when you see a student using techniques from an activity.
- Present the rationale for why the skill is important and explain that this will be the focus for the week. Make it an important part of class.
- Each chapter offers numerous student worksheets, which lend themselves easily to being used on a daily basis. Don't overwhelm students—or yourself—if one a day is not the right pace. The goal is not to provide correct answers; it is to change behavior. Recognizing the appropriate use of a particular skill is a great first step.
- As you guide students through the "social skills time" or whatever you call your sessions, remind them of the skill they are working on.
- Look for examples of good behavior throughout the week. Ask students to point out acceptable examples they see in each other.
- As you discuss the worksheets, make connections for the students between this skill and how it will help them in their daily life.
- As problems or opportunities arise, ask students what skill would be helpful at that time.

I hope that you and your students will find these materials to be helpful and enjoyable!

—Darlene Mannix

Part I

Personality Traits: What Are You Like?

Introductory Comments

Rationale: Every person is unique. Although we are different, as humans we need to be connected to one another on some level, whether it is through a friendship, neighborhood setting, or developing relationships in a group. For some, making connections seems to be effortless—people are drawn to someone with a fun personality, a sympathetic ear, wise counsel, or even just availability. But others, especially those with poor social skills, need a boost or specific training to help them see themselves as others see them, to gain confidence, to learn or improve behaviors, and even to accept themselves as worthy.

This part of the book is divided into two chapters. Chapter 1, "Investigating Personality Traits," covers many personality traits to consider when evaluating one's own tendencies. Although there are many types of personality tests, the purpose of these lessons is to provide a simple platform where students can identify common personality traits.

The first series of worksheets deals with the "big five," or common personality traits that most people would agree are desirable: honesty, kindness, trustworthiness, friendliness, and being hardworking. The students are not asked to officially rate themselves on these, but merely to think about these attributes and what it means to possess them.

The second series of worksheets digs a little deeper into common personality traits that are not really categorized into "right" or "wrong" but can be viewed as a spectrum. Is it wrong to be messy? Is it desirable to be fun-loving rather than serious? Is it okay to enjoy the journey rather than focus on the destination? This series of traits is designed for the students to evaluate their own personality traits without judgment! It is to help the students come up with an informal profile of "What I Am Like." The student is introduced to the idea of a sliding scale with opposite attributes at each end. Again, there is not a moral judgment to be attached to the responses; merely the responses can be used as tools to get the students thinking about where they would place themselves on the spectrum. This information will be useful in later activities.

Chapter 2, "Putting It All Together," is a third set of worksheets designed to help students take the information they compiled from the previous worksheets and come up with general statements or conclusions about themselves.

For example, suppose you see yourself as a creative, procrastinating, peace-loving introvert. What does that have to do with anything? Well, it does matter in that it affects job situations, choice of friends, being aware of what types of people will build you up or what types of people might take advantage of you. It also helps point out which individual skills would really be beneficial to learn and apply in order to meet personal goals. Knowledge is power—and self-knowledge is something that can be used to help an individual at least identify a starting point.

As students go through the worksheets, it is suggested that they keep data on themselves and compile the information at the end of this section so that they can produce an overview of themselves. They should be able to provide an answer to the question, What are you like? Information should include how they see themselves on the major positive personality traits and a few statements about their individual tendencies.

Also included in this chapter is a lesson on verifying student responses. Students may think they are behaving appropriately in a given situation when they are not. A student may decide they are not a leader, but someone else may recognize leadership qualities that just have not yet been developed. Students are asked to verify their responses by obtaining input from other people.

So, as you keep in mind that this is not a scientific assessment, please use the worksheets to have students explore personality traits; discuss what they are personally like, laugh at the examples, and refrain from labeling one end of the line as "good" and the other as "bad."

We are all social beings, and maybe the first person to make peace with, learn about, and care for is yourself! With that as background, the social process can continue to involve interaction with others!

Where to Go for More

If students are interested, there are numerous online personality tests that students can take for fun or introspection.

Truity.com (a variety of personality tests)

teenagesurvival.com (specifically for teens)

16personalities.com (uses the Myers-Briggs types)

Tips for Teachers

Here are some tips for teachers to use in the classroom to help students become aware of ways to sharpen personality skills.

1. *There are many online personality tests that can help students find their personality types.* Enneagramtest.net is one that divides personality types into nine categories. Another is truity.com, which was created by Myers and Briggs and divides personality into sixteen groups. This information can be very helpful to students (and adults) who are curious to know how they would be scored on these well-known tests.
2. *Help students discover their strengths.* You as a teacher see the student in an academic setting and can help point out what you see as their strengths. It doesn't hurt to be reminded of this! Praise them for their achievements when honestly deserved.
3. *Help students be aware of their weaknesses.* This is just a starting point, not something meant to discourage them. Help them decide on a course to improve an area (academically, socially) that you see as needing help. No one has only strengths; we all have things that can be improved. Acknowledgment is the first step.
4. *Provide students with opportunities to develop interests.* The more students read and learn about the world around them, the more topics they will have to talk about. It's a big world out there—what do they want to learn about?
5. *A typical school setting provides a wide variety of people to interact with.* From the principal to the custodian, from many teachers to the school nurse, the counselor, the bus driver, and the lunch room staff. Each interaction is an opportunity for the student to demonstrate a pleasing personality. Students might require a little coaching before entering some of these areas. There's no reason not to thank someone for doing what they do for students.
6. *Encourage your students to ask questions.* They could ask questions about a lesson to help clarify a point or to request more information about the topic. This shows they are aware of what's being discussed and are with you. In classes other than your class, students should also be coached to ask good questions, not, for example, "Will this be on the test?" But "Can you give another example?" or "Could you explain that process?"
7. *If opportunities arise, have students volunteer for class or school projects.* Students can make deliveries, sort messages, help younger students, and so on. Volunteerism is an excellent way to gain a good reputation.
8. *Have students identify a role model and talk about what aspects of that model are intriguing and positive.* Do they admire the dedication of a professional athlete? Or the humor of a stand-up comic? What personality traits are they drawn to?

9. *Encourage students to have an opinion on topics that are important to them or are timely.* When someone asks them, "What's your opinion about . . . ?," will they have enough knowledge about the topic to express an opinion? Can they back up their opinion with facts as well as feelings? "I don't know" is not an opinion! Push your students to do a little research.
10. *Have students practice giving sincere compliments.* Encourage students to find opportunities to genuinely say something nice about someone else and then kindly, authentically say the nice thing. It doesn't have to be outrageous; in fact, sincerity wins out here. "Cute earrings." "Way to hustle in practice!" "I liked your story." It could even be a thumbs up or nod of the head.

Pointers for Parents

Here are some ideas to help your child gain and use attractive personality qualities around the house or community.

1. *Remind your child that inner beauty is the most important piece of their personality.* It doesn't matter so much what you look like; it's what you are like inside that defines a person. Ask them to tell you about the nicest people they have met. Why are these people attractive and kind?
2. *Smile.* Having the appearance of a pleasing personality often includes a facial smile. Even if you don't feel happy, you can still have a pleasant look on your face. A smile doesn't commit you to anything—it's a very small social cue that you can wear with little effort.
3. *Encourage your child to be a better listener.* Even if you and your family are going in many different directions, put time in your day to gather everyone together and spend time listening to each other. Listening means that what the other person is saying is important. Thank your child for listening; say that it was important to you.
4. *Honesty may be the most important personality trait there is.* If someone is known as being honest, that's a pretty high compliment. Talk to your child about what it means to be honest and to live an honest life. Why is this personality trait so important? A caveat: when it is important to refrain from being too honest. Talk about how it is also important to avoid being brutally honest when tact or withholding comments might be a better response.
5. *Demonstrate to your child what it means to be interested in other people.* What are your neighbors like? Do you know their names? Does somebody need a meal or an errand run? Talking to your neighbors does not mean gossip, but rather finding out about other people because they are in your life and together you help form a community. Ask questions, share pleasantries, wave, and so on. Be the nice next door neighbors.
6. *Use a person's name occasionally in normal conversation with that person.* People like to hear their names. When you are introduced to your child's friends, be sure to use their name. When you introduce your child to someone else (especially an adult), coach them to use that person's name a few times.
7. *Pass on compliments about your child to your child.* They may groan and try to look embarrassed, but when someone has noticed something positive about your child and gone to the trouble of mentioning it to you, that's important! That's worth sharing with your child. Someone noticed their good behavior!

8. *Tell your child what you like about the personalities of their friends.* Without being phony, mention the kindness that you saw or the leadership that was demonstrated. You are indicating to your child that they have some pretty good friends.
9. *Playing table games can bring out all kinds of personality traits.* Your child may be a serious video gamer, but there are few kids who don't also enjoy a good board game from time to time. This is a great way to bring families of all ages together. Monopoly, Ticket to Ride, and Codenames are just a few popular games. Remind the group that this is for fun, there will be no sore losers, and you're out to win!
10. *Try to find an optimistic side of things.* No one enjoys being around a complainer. Even if something seems bad at the moment, chances are things will change and it will not be as awful as you think forever. Your child may feel sad, left out, or unable to face all the challenges of the day, but try to find something good in the day, the situation, or even in the child. "I know this is hard for you, but you'll get through it!" "You are a brave person and this challenge is not going to stop you."

These are my parents—they're going to a class reunion so they're cleaner and younger looking than usual.

Chapter 1

Investigating Personality Traits

Skill 1: Identifying the Big Five Personality Traits

INSTRUCTOR PAGE
Rationale: These are personality traits that are generally accepted as desirable.

Worksheet 1: Are You Honest?

Students are to agree or disagree with the level of honesty shown in the examples.
Answer Key:
1. Disagree 2. Agree 3. Agree 4. Disagree

Worksheet 2: Are You Kind?

Students are to select the character in each pair who is showing kindness.
Answer Key:
1. Second 2. First 3. First 4. Second 5. First

Worksheet 3: Are You Trustworthy?

Students are to select items from a list that they feel comfortable doing.
Answer Key: Answers will vary.

Worksheet 4: Are You Friendly?

Students will give a response to show friendliness in situations.
Answer Key:
1. Give a greeting. ("Good morning!") 2. Pass magazines. ("Would you mind passing me a magazine?") 3. Shake hands. ("I'd like you to meet my Aunt Stephanie from Detroit.") 4. Help pick up toys. ("What a fun little boy! What's his name?") 5. Tell the waitress it's fine. ("Hello, nice to see you again. I hope you enjoy your meal.")

Worksheet 5: Are You Hardworking?

Students are to choose the character that is the harder worker in each pair.
Answer Key:
1. Second 2. First 3. First 4. Second

Name____ Date______________

Worksheet 1

Are You Honest?

Read the situations below and circle AGREE or DISAGREE if you think the person is showing honest behavior. If you disagree, what do you think is the problem?

1. Alisha is babysitting for her neighbor. The agreed amount was $10 an hour. Mrs. Marshall left the house at 4:00, and her husband returned at 7:30 PM. He asked how much he owed Alisha. She said she had been at the house for 4 hours.

   AGREE DISAGREE

2. Miguel was filling out a form to join an intramural sports team. One of the questions was whether or not he was passing all of his classes. He knew that he was getting a D in history. He wrote down that he was passing all classes but one, but that he was getting a tutor for help.

   AGREE DISAGREE

A

3. Someone knocked out one of the lights in the boys' bathroom during passing period. Fred saw the boys who did it, but did not want to get in trouble. When the principal asked if he knew anything about it, he said he did not see anything. Later, he told a teacher that he trusted that he did see what happened. The teacher thanked him and said he didn't have to reveal the names because she already had a pretty good idea of who it was.

   AGREE DISAGREE

4. Kenzie was supposed to work at the music store this Saturday, but she got an invitation to go to a baseball game with friends. She told the manager that her grandmother died and she had to go to the funeral and so she couldn't show up for work.

   AGREE DISAGREE

Name________________________________ Date______________

Worksheet 2

Are You Kind?

Which of these students is showing kindness in this situation?

1. Neighbor needs sidewalk shoveled

I hope you don't fall!

I'll get that for you, Mrs. Jones.

2. Little girl can't see the parade going by, too short

Excuse me, this little girl can't see. Could you please move over a little?

MOVE!

Are You Kind? (continued)

3. Man drops his wallet in a store

Hey, you dropped something! You might need this!

Oh! I wonder if there's money!

4. Woman on crutches

Wow, what happened to you?

Can I get the door for you?

5. Person sitting on a park bench, crying

Are you OK? Do you need anything?

I'll just ignore him.

Name____ Date______________

Worksheet 3

Are You Trustworthy?

For which of these situations would you feel comfortable? Put a check mark by those examples.

1. Taking care of the neighbor's dog while they are gone for a week on vacation.
2. Taking care of a newborn baby while the parents go shopping for food for an hour.
3. Remembering to bring in all the outdoor plants before a frost warning.
4. Remembering to transfer the wet clothes to the dryer.
5. Returning a game that you borrowed from a friend for a week.
6. Agreeing to deliver T-shirts to everyone on your team.
7. Paying back a friend who lent you money for snacks at a movie.
8. Closing the garage door and the windows in your house when you see a storm coming.
9. Making sure your little brother/nephew arrives safely at the daycare center in the morning.
10. Keeping a secret about something that is not dangerous or wrong.

Name____ Date______________

Worksheet 4

Are You Friendly?

How could you respond in a friendly manner in the following situations?

1. Person getting on a bus
2. Sitting in a waiting room
3. Being introduced to an adult
4. Kid throwing toys around, while his mother is talking
5. Waitress at a fast food restaurant

Break room

Name____ Date______________

Worksheet 5

Are You Hardworking?

Choose the character in each situation who is demonstrating that they are a hard worker.

1.

This project is taking forever. I'll finish it tomorrow. Or see if my brother will finish it for me.

I'm going to take a break, then get right back to this and get it DONE!

2.

My neighbor wants me to rake all those leaves. It will take hours. I'll time myself and see how fast I can get it done.

He is paying me by the hour. I'll rake really slowly!!

Are You Hardworking? (continued)

3.

I was supposed to clean up my bedroom. I'll go ahead and clean the bathroom too since I have all the cleaner stuff out anyhow.
My bedroom is a mess. I'll throw everything under the bed and call it good!

4.

I'm so tired of typing! I think this short story that I wrote for English will get me by. It's supposed to be short anyhow, right?
I think I could make this story better if I changed some things. I know I can do a better job if I put more time into it.

Skill 2: Identifying Yourself on Common Personality Traits: How You Function in a Group Setting

INSTRUCTOR PAGE

Rationale: When placed in a group setting, some individuals prefer to take a leadership role while others work best as teammates. When evaluating oneself, it's important to consider factors such as how one works with ideas and how one handles criticism.

On Worksheets 6–25, students are to rate themselves on a continuum at the bottom of each worksheet. They can place a mark to indicate how they see themselves on each trait.

Worksheet 6: Lead or Follow

Students are to evaluate themselves as far as leader/follower tendencies when given a group task. Students should rate themselves on the line at the bottom.

Questions: 1. In what situations have you shown leadership? 2. Do you get anxious and worried when given a leadership role? 3. Are you told that you have good ideas and find that others follow them?
Answer Key: Answers will vary.

Worksheet 7: Micromanage or Let Go

The situations on this worksheet help the student to decide if they are able to manage others in a leadership role or if they are uncomfortable with details not being exactly correct. Students should rate themselves on the line at the bottom. Note: micromanaging is not meant to be a negative characteristic; rather, it emphasizes checking for details that might not be important, depending on the task.

Questions: 1. Do you trust others to do the job they are given, or do you feel responsible for making sure it is done correctly? 2. Do you get irritated when you feel that someone is looking over your shoulder, always inspecting your work? 3. Are you able to let it go if the job or task is not going well but not really endangering anyone?
Answer Key:

1. Micromanaging 2. Micromanaging 3. Micromanaging 4. Let go

Worksheet 8: Working Alone or with Others

Given a choice, students can indicate if they prefer to work in a group or complete a task on their own. Students should rate themselves on the line at the bottom.

Questions: 1. In what type of situations do you like to work alone? 2. In what situations do you prefer to work as part of a group? 3. What are the advantages of each type? 4. Do you prefer one over the other?

Answers will vary.

Worksheet 9: Introduce New Ideas or Wait to Be Asked

Students are to read the story and discuss if they share ideas easily or withhold them unless prompted. Students should rate themselves on the line at the bottom.

Questions: 1. Do you think Saanvi would have given her ideas if Theo had specifically asked her? 2. Why do you think she was hesitant to contribute? 3. Are there other ways Saanvi could let her ideas be known?

Worksheet 10: Accept or Resent Criticism

Students are to read about several situations and decide if the main character resents or accepts criticism. Students should rate themselves on the line at the bottom.

Questions: 1. Have you ever been criticized unfairly? Explain. 2. Did criticism ever cause you to work harder to succeed? 3. Do you think the person criticizing you has any right to comment on your behavior or skill?

Answer Key:

1. Accept 2. Resent 3. Resent 4. Resent

Name____ Date______________

Worksheet 6

Lead or Follow

Where do you see yourself in these situations? As a leader of the project/situation or as someone who helps carry out the details?

1. Your class of 35 students is supposed to come with a school-wide program to present information on bullying. What would you like to do to help?

2. You and four others are given the job of delivering 100 boxes of cookies all over the neighborhood. What will you do first?

3. Your name came up as someone who could run for class president. Your duties would be overseeing all of the school issues that go with your class as well as coming up with ideas to promote class projects. How do you feel about that?

4. There are two teams involved in friendly Olympics in your neighborhood. Do you want to be the captain of one of the teams?

LEADER		SOMETIMES		PREFER TO FOLLOW DIRECTIONS
5	4	3	2	1

Name________________________________ Date____________

Worksheet 7

Micromanage or Let Go

Read these situations and decide if the main character is micromanaging (stuck on details) or if they let things go appropriately. Think about what you would do in each situation.

1. Ben was supposed to check in every poster that was submitted for a school contest. Each poster should have the student's name, class, and date written on the back. As he went through the posters, Ben put aside the ones that were missing information so he could find the missing information later.
2. Callista wanted all of the cheerleaders to wear their hair exactly the same with an orange ribbon in their hair, orange socks, and two pompoms. Jessica was running late and forgot the hair ribbon. Abbi didn't get the message and wore white socks. Callista didn't think they should cheer for the game that night because they didn't follow the dress code.
3. Deshawn was pouring lemonade for a class party of about 70 people. He was told not to fill the cups to the top because it might spill. He asked two other students to help fill the cups, but he wanted them to pour 2/3 of the cup. The other students were filling them only about halfway. Deshawn added lemonade to all of the cups that were not filled to the 2/3 mark.
4. At work, the team leader asked Randy to have all of the other employees wash their equipment before leaving their shift. Randy watched two or three of them wash and then decided to leave because it seemed like they were getting the job done without being watched.

MICROMANAGER		SOMETIMES		CAN LET THINGS GO
5	4	3	2	1

Name____ Date____________

Worksheet 8

Working Alone or with Others

Which of these situations makes you feel most comfortable?

1.

OK kids, form groups of 10 each!

2.

Here's the project—get to work on your own!

3.

Find a partner and then we will start the lab. You'll turn in one paper and share the grade.

4.

We need to design scenery for the play. Girls, do the background. Boys, design the house interior.

Working Alone or with Others (continued)

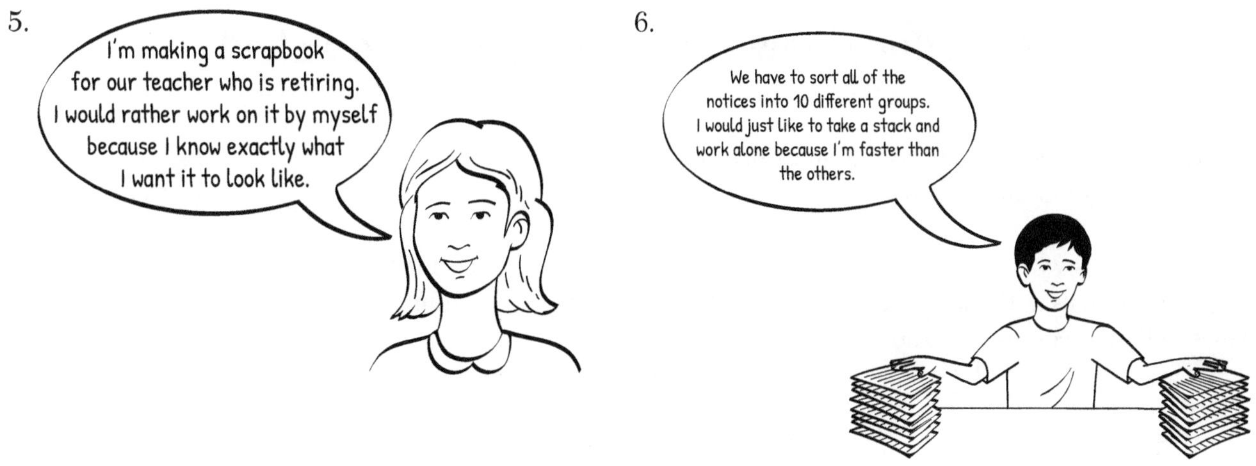
5.
I'm making a scrapbook for our teacher who is retiring. I would rather work on it by myself because I know exactly what I want it to look like.
6.
We have to sort all of the notices into 10 different groups. I would just like to take a stack and work alone because I'm faster than the others.

ALONE		BOTH		GROUP
5	4	3	2	1

Name____ Date______________

Worksheet 9

Introduce New Ideas or Wait to Be Asked

Read the story and respond to the questions at the end. Try to think about what you might do in this situation.

Saanvi was working on a group project to promote awareness of adopting stray animals at the local animal shelter. The group gathered to think of ways to let the community know about adopting animals.

Theo was the leader of the project and gathered the other students together to share ideas.

"I think we should have some visual art to attract people's attention," he said. "What are some ways we could get people to know about the needs?"

Saanvi thought about how she loved to take pictures and had some great filters on her camera. It would look amazing to have posters with cute pictures of dogs and cats smiling into the camera!

"Hey, I know," said Candace. "Why don't we post pictures of the dogs and cats on Facebook and Instagram?"

"Great idea," said Theo. "Who else has ideas?"

Saanvi thought it would also be helpful to have guided tours of the shelter on Saturdays so people could come and see the facilities. But maybe someone else had a better idea.

"What if we walked the dogs on leashes around the community center and let people see them?" volunteered Alexa.

"Another great idea," said Theo. "This group is really thinking!"

"I guess they don't need my ideas," thought Saanvi. "They are doing just fine without me."

SPEAK UP		DEPENDS		WAIT TO BE ASKED
5	4	3	2	1

Name____ Date______________

Worksheet 10

Accept or Resent Criticism

Read the following situations. Decide if the individual resents the criticism or is accepting of it. Circle your answer next to each example.

1. "The boss said I came in late way too many times last month and I better start getting here on time and to work better as a team. He doesn't know all that I have to do before I can show up to work. But I want to keep this job, so I'll adjust things to get to work on time."

   ACCEPT RESENT

2. "I can't believe my English teacher thought our whole class was doing a sloppy job of proofreading our written work. Then she used an example from MY PAPER to demonstrate how NOT to start a paragraph. She said she wasn't even going to read anything unless we turned in a rough draft first. Yes, I did rush through, but that's her job, isn't it? To read it anyway? I just want to get it done."

   ACCEPT RESENT

3. "No one in this group seemed to like my ideas. In fact, Tomas said my ideas were very immature and would only appeal to children. I'm through giving ideas. I'll just shut up—even though I know my ideas are great."

   ACCEPT RESENT

4. "Coach was really disappointed in our basketball practice today. He said we weren't trying very hard. But we were! None of us wants to play for him anymore. I'm going to quit the team. I thought I was trying as hard as I could."

   ACCEPT RESENT

ACCEPT CRITICISM				RESENT CRITICISM
5	4	3	2	1

Skill 3: Identifying Yourself on Common Personality Traits: How You Organize Things

INSTRUCTOR PAGE

Rationale: Most people have their own system of organizing things—objects, ideas, tasks, and so on. On the one hand, a particular organizational system may look quite chaotic, but if it works for the individual, who's to criticize? On the other hand, if other people need to operate in the same physical space, it might call for agreed-on structure.

Worksheet 11: Visually in Place or Looks Chaotic

After viewing two different systems of organization, the student will analyze parts of each that they like or dislike. Students should rate themselves on the line at the bottom.

Answers will vary.

Questions: 1. Which parts of Julia's organization method did you like? Dislike? 2. What did you think of Alfonso's room and organization ideas? 3. How would you characterize your own organizational methods? Think about objects, tasks, ideas, and so on.

Worksheet 12: Big Picture or Detail-Oriented

Students are to sort examples into which are big-picture tasks and which focus on details. Students should rate themselves on the line at the bottom.

Answer Key:

1. Big 2. Detail 3. Detail 4. Big 5. Detail 6. Big 7. Could be either; how much snow? 8. Big 9. Could be either; how many tests are given? 10. Big

Questions: 1. What are some of your big-picture tasks or goals? 2. What are some details that make up your big picture? 3. Are you more comfortable chipping away at smaller tasks before taking on a bigger goal?

Worksheet 13: Planner or Spontaneous

Students are given examples to categorize as planned (put some thought into ahead of time) or spontaneous (go with feelings of the moment). Students should rate themselves on the line at the bottom.

Answer Key:

1. Planner 2. Spontaneous 3. Spontaneous 4. Planner 5. Spontaneous 6. Planner 7. Spontaneous 8. Planner 9. Spontaneous 10. Planner

Questions: 1. What are some advantages to being a planner? 2. What is attractive about being spontaneous? 3. What might be frustrating if a planner and a spontaneous person were working together on a task?

Worksheet 14: Own or Delegate

Some individuals prefer to split a project into parts and have others do a share; others want to own the entire project and control every aspect of it. Students should rate themselves on the line at the bottom.

Answer Key:

1. Own 2. Own 3. Delegate 4. Own 5. Delegate

Questions: 1. When you take on a project, do you prefer to complete it entirely on your own? 2. When it is helpful to delegate jobs to other people? 3. In general, do you like to be the owner of the task, or can you give up pieces of it to others?

Worksheet 15: Ask for Help or Figure It Out

Students may prefer a style of problem-solving that involves figuring something out; they like to analyze the situation and solve the problem on their own. Others go straight to asking for help. On this activity, A = asking for help and O = on my own. Students should rate themselves on the line at the bottom.

Answers will vary.

Questions: 1. Do you tend to ask for help because a job seems too big or because you are not sure how to complete it? 2. Do you like to solve problems on your own because you like to figure things out? 3. Are there times when you know you could solve a problem, but just don't want to? Why?

Name____ Date____________

Worksheet 11

Visually in Place or Looks Chaotic

Take a tour of the rooms of Julia and Alfonso. Which parts can you relate to? Which room is most like yours?

Julia's Room:

I like to see everything that I've got, so I don't like boxes and drawers. My jewelry is in a bowl and I can dig through it to find my accessories for the day!

You can see that my books, bag, and laptop are on the floor, right next to my bed where I can get to them. Sometimes I trip over them, but it just reminds me that I still have things to do with them.

My TO-DO list is taped to my mirror so I'll see it every morning!

I have a few art projects that aren't quite ready to be turned in, so they are accessible to me. Why would I put them away when I'm just going to get them out again? Sometimes I can't find my brushes, but I know they'll turn up eventually. I found one in my jewelry bowl!

My clothes are stacked in order of how I took them off. I'll throw them in the laundry on the weekend. If I have the time. I might need my hiking sticks for a trip this weekend, but I know exactly where they are . . .. in the back of the closet, under some boxes!

Usually I'm in a hurry when I'm doing anything, so I like to spend my time doing things, rather than putting things away! As long as I can find what I need, what's wrong with that?

Visually in Place or Looks Chaotic (continued)

Alfonso's Room:

I like the feel of open space. I put all my clothes on hangers or in a drawer so I can get to them easily. And, NO, I don't label everything—I know that socks and underwear are in the top drawer (socks to the left, underwear to the right), T-shirts in the middle drawer, and jeans on the bottom. I fold everything so nothing gets wrinkled.

I collect rocks. I have all kinds of interesting specimens and I like to look at them and display them on a shelf. I also have a lot of trophies, but I don't like to crowd the shelf so I put them in a different place. My dad and I built a corner case and I put them there.

There's a big desk that I use for my computer and all my other school projects and materials. It might look messy, but everything is in a stack according to what the class or project needs. My phone is always charged at night right next to the lamp so I'm all set for the next day. My Xbox is in the corner with a couple of comfy chairs. Games are stacked in a container.

My TO-DO list is on my computer and I check it every morning to see what I need to take care of each day.

Trash day is on Thursdays, so I make sure my wastebasket is emptied and taken out the night before. Sometimes I do eat in my room, and I can't stand seeing black banana peels or candy wrappers. So out they go, as soon as possible!

I do like to know that I can get to anything I need quickly and easily; I don't have to hunt for anything. My sister, Julia, laughs at me because I spend time putting things in place. But her room—well, you've seen it!

IN A SPECIFIC PLACE				LOOKS CHAOTIC
5	4	3	2	1

Name________________________________ Date_______________

Worksheet 12

Big Picture or Detail-Oriented

Some people like to focus on the whole picture when working on a task or goal, whereas others focus on the details that make it happen. Which of the items below are big picture and which are details?

1. We need to clean the entire house before company comes. _______________
2. When shopping, I have to pick up bananas and ketchup. _______________
3. I need to clean out the paintbrushes before I can paint my room. _______________
4. Let's have a party for your birthday next week! _______________
5. We will need to send out special invitations to the guests for your party! ____________
6. I'm going to write a book about my life. ___________________

Story

7. We have to shovel the driveway after this snowstorm. _______________
8. I'm going to get my high school diploma by next year! ____________
9. I wonder if I'm going to pass the next geometry test. ____________
10. I'm going to apply for a job so I can save up for college. ___________

BIG PICTURE				DETAILS
5	4	3	2	1

Name____ Date______________

Worksheet 13

Planner or Spontaneous

Some people are planners; they like to think ahead about what could or might happen in a situation. Others take a more spontaneous approach to what's ahead of them. They do not worry about what's coming but react to situations as they come. Which of the following statements sounds like you?

1. When I go on a trip, I think about where I'm going, what I'll need to take, where I will stay, and what I will do.
2. I'm writing a story, but I have no idea how it will end! I'm letting the characters experience things and add to the plot as I go.

3. When I go bike riding, I like to just get on my bike and go!

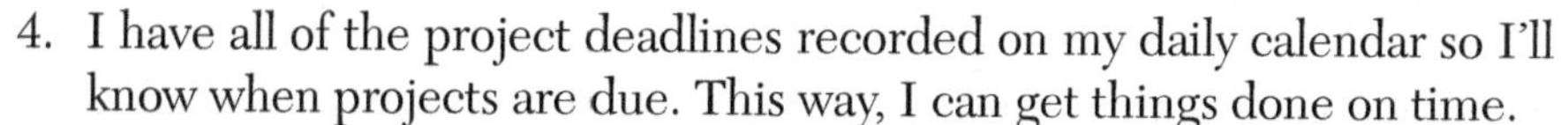

4. I have all of the project deadlines recorded on my daily calendar so I'll know when projects are due. This way, I can get things done on time.
5. When I get together with my good friends, we don't decide what we're going to do until we are actually together.
6. I check the upcoming weather before I decide what I'm going to wear.
7. I like to listen to the music on my playlist in a random order.
8. If someone has something to sell me, I want to think about it first and do a little research to see if it's something I really need.
9. If I go to a pet store, I'll probably come home with a puppy!
10. If I have to give a speech, I'll practice it over and over until I feel very comfortable with it!

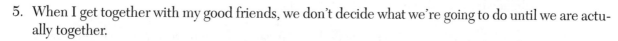

PLANNER				SPONTANEOUS
5	4	3	2	1

Name____ Date______________

Worksheet 14

Own or Delegate

The following characters are working on projects or have a task to complete. Which ones are demonstrating ownership and which are delegating?

1. Our community is letting us paint a mural on the side of a building. I have a great idea for a giant butterfly. I know exactly what I want it to look like.
2. I want to design and display a flag that represents our school. I have researched the history of our school community.
3. I'm in charge of hosting an authentic Spanish meal for our Spanish club. I'm going to look for volunteers to bring utensils, ingredients, napkins, and decorations. Some of the people in class can set up chairs and take them down when we're done.
4. I am writing a play about the founding of our town. It's fictional, but I think it will be really interesting. I already have an idea of how I want it to end.
5. Time for the annual Talent Show! I signed up our garage band to perform. I will pick the song, but I'll need help with costumes, running sound, and scheduling rehearsals.

I really appreciate your help!

OWN A TASK				DELEGATE
5	4	3	2	1

Name______________________________ Date______________

Worksheet 15

Ask for Help or Figure It Out

Sometimes people get stuck in a situation and have a problem to take care of. Do you see yourself asking for help in these situations or would you tend to figure it out on your own?

A = ask for help
O = on my own

1. Your bike has a flat tire. There are some tools and a spare tube in the bike kit.
2. You need something in a storage box on the top shelf in your basement. You can't reach it.
3. The printer is out of paper.
4. Your computer is not online. There was a big storm last night.
5. You know there's a big math test coming up but you don't remember when it is. Usually your tests are on Fridays.
6. You're trying to put together a chair but the assembly instructions don't seem to go with this particular chair.
7. You planned to walk the dog but someone must have moved his leash from its usual place.
8. The neighbor's trash blew into your front yard and into the street in front of your driveway. It's a lot of trash!

ASK FOR HELP				FIGURE IT OUT
5	4	3	2	1

Skill 4: Identifying Yourself on Common Personality Traits: How You Make Decisions

INSTRUCTOR PAGE

Rationale: People process making decisions differently. At one end, there are people who are more methodical, who seek advice and prefer to weigh all aspects of the decision. At the other end are people who like to make decisions quickly, using emotion, past experiences, and other factors.

Worksheet 16: Quick Decision or Think It Over

Students are to decide which in each pair of characters is making a quick decision or thinking it over. Students should rate themselves on the line at the bottom.

Answer Key:

1. A—thinking B—quick 2. A—quick B—thinking 3. A—thinking B—quick 4. A—thinking B—quick

Questions: 1. Do you feel stressed when you have to make a decision in a hurry? 2. Do you prefer to think things over before committing to something, even if it's not a relatively important decision? 3. Have you had an experience in which making a quick decision was the right decision? Explain.

Worksheet 17: Regret Mistakes or Accept and Move On

Students are to give advice to each of the characters who has made a mistake or has a regret. Students should rate themselves on the line at the bottom.

Answer Key:

1. Try to laugh about it. 2. Ask brother to help pay to replace the laptop. 3. Look for a part-time job. 4. Let haircut grow out. 5. Keep trying to find new things to talk about.

Answers may vary.

Questions: 1. Think about a mistake that you may have regretted. Did you find a way to move on or do you still think about the situation? 2. Do you feel that you need to punish yourself (or someone else) for the mistake? Why do you feel that way, if so? 3. Sometimes mistakes work themselves out, but the lesson learned remains. Does this help you feel better about handling future situations that might be risky?

Worksheet 18: Get Advice or Make a Good Guess

Students should decide which situations might benefit from getting advice from someone. Students should rate themselves on the line at the bottom.

Answer Key:

1. Advice 2. Guess 3. Advice 4. Guess 5. Guess 6. Advice 7. Advice 8. Advice 9. Advice 10. Advice

Questions: 1. In each of the cases on the worksheet, what is the worst that could happen if you just took a guess rather than ask for advice? What if you guessed wrong? 2. In each case, who is a person who could give helpful advice? 3. Do you prefer to ask other people for input or do you prefer to make a good guess when making a decision?

Worksheet 19: Weigh Pros and Cons or Go with Gut

On this sheet, students should provide an example of a pro and a con for each situation. Students should rate themselves on the line at the bottom.

Answer Key:

1. Make money/give up free time. 2. Have someone to spend time with/have to put time into a relationship. 3. Feel better/risk injury. 4. Make space in closet/give up memories. 5. Get advice/reveal personal feelings. 6. Works well/costs money. 7. Get fit/costs time and money. 8. Beautiful tank/might be difficult to maintain. 9. Pride when finished/time and energy involved. 10. Make a new friend/might give up activities you want to do on your own.

Answers may vary.

Questions: 1. Is it difficult to think of both a pro and a con for many decisions? 2. Do you ever try to convince yourself that what you really want is the right decision, even if you realize there is a down side? 3. What are some decisions you are thinking about now? Does a pro/con system help organize your thinking? 4. What are some decisions that you might make that are going with your gut rather than systematically thinking through all sides? 5. What are some situations that would require a gut reaction in a hurry?

Worksheet 20: Opportunities or Disasters

Students should identify a way that each character found something good about a seemingly bad situation. Students should rate themselves on the line at the bottom.

Answer Key:

1. Got a more suitable job 2. Waited and got a better deal 3. Found out she enjoyed a different activity more 4. Gained experience and reputation for caring for special needs animal

Questions: 1. Can you think of examples when you (or someone you know) made a decision that did not turn out the way they had hoped? 2. Are you more likely to see mistakes as disasters when they really might just be getting off track a little?

Name____ Date______________

Worksheet 16

Quick Decision or Think It Over

Here are some decisions that these students have to make. Which student is making a quick decision and which is thinking it over?

1. There is a part-time job working at a lousy restaurant, late hours, with low pay. Ready to hire right now.

A.

I think I'll apply at other places first.

B.

I need the money.
I'll take it for now.

2. There's a party on Saturday at the home of someone you don't know very well.

A.

Sounds fun,
YES.

B.

I don't know if
there will be drinking.
I will talk to some
friends first.

Quick Decision or Think It Over (continued)

3. There is a great deal on a very expensive sound system. Only one left in stock.

A.

It's a lot of
money.
I'm not sure.

B.

It's exactly what
I want! I must
have it.

4. If you can leave right now, you can go on an adventure weekend with some of your friends at a camp. There was a cancellation and now there's room for one more.

A.

I need to check
my work schedule.

B.

I'll make it work!
I'm going.

QUICK DECISION				THINK IT OVER
5	4	3	2	1

Name____ Date____________

Worksheet 17

Regret Mistakes or Accept and Move On

Each of the characters below made some kind of mistake or did something that they now regret. What would you tell each of them? How could they move on?

1. I got a tattoo on my ankle. It didn't turn out very well. Now I wish I hadn't done that.
2. My brother borrowed my laptop and dropped it in the lake while he was boating. What was he even doing with my laptop in a boat?
3. I talked my parents into letting me get a smartphone that I really couldn't afford. Now I have to make payments every month, and it's hard.
4. I let my friend's sister's cousin cut my hair. Just look at it. I'll need to wear a hat for months.
5. I wish I had not told my grandmother that I didn't want to work in the family business after high school. Now she shames me every time I see her, and it's all she wants to talk about when we're together.

REGRET				ACCEPT
5	4	3	2	1

Name____ Date_____________

Worksheet 18

Get Advice or Make a Good Guess

Which of these situations could best be solved by getting advice from someone? Which might be resolved by making a good guess?

1. Deciding how people should be invited to a very formal wedding.
2. Deciding how many people should be invited to a party at your house.
3. Needing to know how much it costs to go on a spring break trip with a group.
4. Finding out how much it costs to get a manicure/haircut.
5. Locating the best deal on new shoes.
6. Deciding how to wash a pile of very dirty clothes.
7. Deciding whether or not to bring home a stray cat with five kittens.
8. Having a very bad toothache.
9. Cooking using some old food that is smelling rather odd.
10. Preparing a meal for someone who has a lot of food allergies.

ADVICE				GUESS
5	4	3	2	1

Name________________________________ Date______________

Worksheet 19

Weigh Pros and Cons or Go with Gut

Making a decision about something usually involves predicting the outcome from both sides—the pro side (it's a good decision) or the con side (it's not best for me). Are you able to see both positive and negative sides of these situations?

	PRO	CON
1. Getting a part-time job.		
2. Having a girlfriend/boyfriend.		
3. Joining a sport team.		
4. Selling equipment you don't use anymore.		
5. Talking to a counselor.		
6. Buying a newer computer or laptop.		
7. Joining a gym.		
8. Having a salt water aquarium.		
9. Taking on a huge project at school.		
10. Hanging out with someone who is unpopular.		

You did really a nice job on mowing the lawn.

SEE BOTH SIDES .... EMPHASIZE ONE OR OTHER

5 4 3 2 1

Name____ Date______________

Worksheet 20

Opportunities or Disasters

Even an unhelpful decision can still lead to something good! You can salvage something from a situation if you can view it as an opportunity rather than a disaster. How did these characters find something redeeming in their situations?

1. Sherman decided to drop out of school because he found it too hard to complete classwork with his ADHD. He eventually got a job working at a factory assembling boat parts and no one could keep up with him! He loved to stay moving, stay busy, and work on his feet.
2. Alan's neighbor offered to sell him a used car for not very much money. He loved the car, but couldn't come up with the money and decided to pass on the opportunity. A few months later, a friend of the family gave him a much nicer car that they didn't need anymore. He was glad he waited!

3. Keisha did not get picked to join the cheerleader squad, even though she was a good athlete. She decided to work on her gymnastic skills instead and was quite successful. The following year, she didn't even try out for cheerleading because she was having so much fun being a gymnast.
4. Laurence decided to get a very old dog from the animal shelter. He knew it was not in good health, but he decided to give the guy a home for life. When Rocky passed away, Laurence was heartbroken, but he knew that what he had done was the right thing. The animal shelter called him soon after and had a young puppy that needed a home. They did not even need to call about references for Laurence.

OPPORTUNITIES				DISASTERS
5	4	3	2	1

Skill 5: Identifying Yourself on Common Personality Traits: Your General Demeanor/ What You're Mostly Like

INSTRUCTOR PAGE

Rationale: These worksheets provide the student with a few general attributes to consider that describe what they are like in very broad categories. These attributes could fill in the blank: "In general, I'm a ______ person." (quiet, creative, sensitive, and so on) There are, of course, many other characteristics that could be included.

Worksheet 21: Outgoing or Quiet

Students are directed to put a check mark next to the items on the list that best describe themselves. Students should rate themselves on the line at the bottom.

Answers will vary.

Questions: 1. Did you have more of the odd-numbered (quiet) responses or even-numbered (outgoing)? 2. Do you think of yourself as being primarily a quiet person or outgoing? Or somewhere in between? 3. Are there some situations in which you are the opposite of your usual demeanor?

Worksheet 22: Open to New Ideas or Prefer the Familiar

Students are to identify which situations on the worksheet would best describe them—as preferring to learn something new or preferring the familiar. Students should rate themselves on the line at the bottom.

Answers will vary.

Questions: 1. Are you usually eager or receptive to learning something new? 2. What might prevent you from wanting to try a new way to do something? 3. When has your old or usual method of doing something proven to be the better way?

Worksheet 23: Creative or Structural Thinker

Students should mark each item as C—showing creativity or S—following structure. Students should rate themselves on the line at the bottom.

Answer Key:

1. S 2. S 3. C 4. S 5. C 6. C 7. C 8. C

Questions: 1. Do you enjoy classes or experiences involving art, music, writing, drama, or dance? Are there other artistic expressions that you enjoy? 2. Do you enjoy the discipline of working on a project or skill and finding out that you are improving with practice, even if it's the same task over and over?

Worksheet 24: Hold Grudges or Quick to Forgive

Students will identify who is having a hard time giving up their grudges. Students should rate themselves on the line at the bottom.

Answer Key:

1. Grudge 2. Grudge 3. Grudge 4. Grudge 5. Grudge 6. Responded by talking to his father

Questions: 1. Why is it hard to forgive people when you have been hurt by someone? 2. Do you think that holding a grudge helps you in any way? 3. What relationships were damaged in the examples on the worksheet?

Worksheet 25: Sensitive to Others or Not into Feelings

Students are to identify the characters who are showing sensitivity to others. Students should rate themselves on the line at the bottom.

Answer Key:

1. Insensitive 2. Sensitive 3. Sensitive 4. Insensitive 5. Insensitive 6. Sensitive 7. Sensitive 8. Sensitive

Questions: 1. Is it always important to talk about your feelings? 2. Is it important to be sensitive to others who might have an unusual situation and might not want to talk about it? 3. Which category best describes you most of the time?

Name______________________________ Date__________

Worksheet 21

Outgoing or Quiet

Which of these characteristics describe you? Put a check mark by the ones that appeal to you.

1. I would rather listen to other people's conversations than be a part of them.
2. I usually have something to say about anything!
3. I express myself in writing rather than speaking.

4. I like to join in fun group activities.
5. I enjoy watching activities rather than getting involved in them.
6. I'm the one who wants to perform for others in a show or event.
7. I would rather work behind the scenes in a project than be directing it.
8. It doesn't bother me at all to speak in front of people I don't know.
9. I have a lot of ideas but I don't always share them.
10. I'm the first to raise my hand to volunteer for anything—I don't even care what it is I'm volunteering for.
11. I think best when I'm alone or in a quiet place.

Outgoing or Quiet (continued)

12. If there's a bunch of people laughing and yelling, I want to be a part of it.
13. People are always telling me to speak up!
14. I'll strike up a conversation with someone whom I don't know on a bus or in a group.
15. I have one or two close friends.
16. People seem to want to hang out with me—I'm rarely alone and that's fine with me.

OUTGOING				QUIET
5	4	3	2	1

Name ______________________ Date ____________

Worksheet 22

Open to New Ideas or Prefer the Familiar

In which of these situations would you prefer to learn something new? In which would you rather stick to what you already know?

1. A friend told you about downloading an app that will help you track how much time you spend walking your dog. You have to do some setup to make it work easily. You usually just put a check mark on a calendar for every day that you walk your dog. You really don't need to know how many minutes you walked, but it might be interesting to know!

2. You are driving your uncle's new car for a week while he's on vacation. It has so much new technology on it that your head is spinning! It practically drives itself. Uncle Max said he would be glad to show you how to operate everything if you are interested.

3. There are some shortcuts that will help you memorize some terminology in your biology class. You already have a system that works for you that will help you on a test. But maybe these shortcuts would be helpful in other classes.

4. You have been riding your horse for years for fun. You enjoy trail riding, jumping over a few logs, and hanging out with other equestrian friends. A new boarder in your barn said there is an instructor who will come to teach anyone at the barn who is interested in some new things to do with your horse. Is it time to listen to what she has to say?

LEARN NEW THINGS				PREFER USUAL WAY
5	4	3	2	1

Name____________________________________ Date____________

Worksheet 23

Creative or Structural Thinker

Which of these characters is showing creativity? Mark them with a C. Which are following structured rules or guidelines? Mark them with an S. Which situations do you relate to the most?

1. Nia got a paint-by-number kit for her birthday. She likes how it's so easy to make a beautiful painting—by herself! __________

2. Min-jin follows the list very carefully when he's babysitting the neighbor's children. Dinner at 5, play outside at 6, bedtime at 7. __________
3. Hannah throws away recipes and throws in a little of this, a little of that, and tastes the food as she makes it. It never comes out the same, but it's always good. __________
4. Jefferson enjoys reading mysteries because they often have clues to follow. He likes to analyze what's happening and try to solve the problems. __________
5. When Natasha redecorates her bedroom, it's totally changed. She rearranges the furniture, paints the walls, changes all the colors, and adds weird pieces of decoration that she has found in odd places. __________
6. Leon loves to write poetry and short stories. He spends time thinking about unusual words to use and how to put twists and turns in his stories. __________
7. Alan doesn't build snowmen in the winter; he builds snow forts, snow camels, and snow castles that are big enough for kids to play in. __________
8. Elizabeth loves to babysit. She comes prepared with crazy games for the kids to play and makes up stories to tell them before they go to bed. __________

CREATIVE				STRUCTURE
5	4	3	2	1

Name________________________________ Date____________

Worksheet 24

Hold Grudges or Quick to Forgive

When someone has hurt or wronged you, do you forgive and forget or are you likely to hold a grudge? Which of these characters is responding appropriately, in your opinion? Discuss.

1. I'm still mad at Bob. He borrowed my canoe and then put a hole in it! He didn't even offer to patch it. I'm not letting him borrow anything else of mine until he apologizes and makes it right. I don't care if he is my best friend.
2. I found out Danielle has been talking about me behind my back. She said she was sorry and that it wasn't really anything important. Still, I'm taking her off my birthday party list. I don't care how much she cries.
3. I do not speak to my neighbors. They called the police on us when we were just playing ball in the empty yard. They said we were noisy and disrespectful. We will keep playing whenever we want to and not be quick about cleaning up our trash in that area.
4. The teacher said my paragraph was a poor example of writing. Well, I'm done. I don't care if he didn't like it.
5. I have never liked Kevin. He called me fat when I was in first grade. It was a long time ago, but I will not forget that remark.
6. My father really embarrassed me in front of my friends. I do not like to be teased. I'll ask him to please stop.

HOLD GRUDGE				FORGIVE
5	4	3	2	1

Name____ Date____________

Worksheet 25

Sensitive to Others or Not into Feelings

Which of the following characters are sensitive to others? Which characters seem insensitive to others' feelings?

1. "Hey, join the team! Grab a T-shirt and you can be on the blue team. I heard your dad just lost his job. Sorry about that. Let's go so we can get the best court."
2. "Maria had a dermatology appointment this morning and her face is all swollen. Don't make a big deal about it because she's already embarrassed."
3. "I know you've been worried about something. You don't have to talk about it if you don't want to, but I'm here if you need anything."
4. "Your dog died? Let me tell you about when MY dog died. Here, sit down, this is going to take a while. When he was a puppy . . . ."
5. "My brother broke up with his latest girlfriend. Now he will be moping around the house and won't want to do anything. He always gets like this. It's such a pain."
6. "Hey, this is Arnaud. He is an exchange student from France. Let's make sure we include him in our activities. He doesn't know anyone, and his English is pretty good but could use some work."
7. "Oh no, I forgot Allie has peanut allergies, and here we are having all kinds of food with nuts in it. I'll make sure there are alternative snacks for her."
8. "My mom keeps wanting me to talk about how I feel after losing the race. I'd just like to move on and not talk about it at all. But I know she means well, so I'll tell her I'm OK."

SENSITIVE				NOT INTO FEELINGS
5	4	3	2	1

Chapter 2

Putting It All Together

Chapter 2

Putting It All Together

INSTRUCTOR PAGES

Worksheet 26: Verifying Your Responses

Students are to check their personality information against comments and feedback from other sources, namely, other people, candid people, and self-observation.

Questions: 1. Why is it important to include input from others when you are trying to assess your personality traits? 2. Do you think it can be a little uncomfortable or surprising to hear comments made about yourself? 3. When you look back at your behavior over the past months or even years, what changes have you observed in your personality? 4. How do these factors affect changes in your personality over time: life experiences, pleasant or unpleasant encounters with other people, adjusting to new situations, being successful at something, learning new skills, maturing?

Worksheet 27: Your Personality Profile

Students are to review their responses to the various personality attributes and select at least one main response from each of the four groups. They can then add one personal or special detail. This should give them at least five sentences that they can put together to make a descriptive paragraph.

Questions: 1. Do you feel that you have a better understanding of what your personality is like? 2. Are you able to describe attributes of your personality in a few thoughtful sentences? 3. Would it help to practice giving a short description of yourself, using this information?

Worksheet 28: Why Personality Matters

Students are to match five reasons why knowing your personality is important with the examples.

Answer Key: 1. C (Mike can try learning hip hop.) 2. A (Might want to avoid the child-friendly showing of the movie) 3. E (Theo is a creative designer and will do a great job on the float.) 4. D (They can learn from Roberto's negotiating techniques.) 5. B (Lucia will enjoy being with the other swimmers.)

Questions: 1. What are some situations that you may have avoided because you weren't sure how you would handle them? 2. Do you find that you like to hang out with people whose personality is similar to yours? Or very different? Or both?

Worksheet 29: Job/Task Match with Your Personality

Students are to decide whether or not the job/task would be a good match for each character.

Answer Key: 1. No, Zoe may be too shy to be a tour guide for a group of people. 2. Yes, Jimmy likes to research details. 3. Yes, Adrienne would probably have a lot of fun with this group. 4. No, if others have to help out in this project they might have trouble understanding what Liam wants it to look like. 5. No, this could be a job situation in which Philip could have rude customers.

Questions: 1. Which characters do you think will have trouble on the job? 2. What jobs or tasks might be better suited for those individuals?

Worksheet 30: Can You Change Your Personality?

Students are given a list of ways that they might enhance some of their personality traits.

Questions: 1. How has your personality changed over the past few years? 2. What traits do you think will always be part of you? 3. Can you think of some other ways to change some personality traits?

Name____ Date______________

Worksheet 26

Verifying Your Responses

Do you know people who talk nonstop but insist they are great listeners? Or refuse to take criticism because they are always right? Here are some ways to help make sure that what you think of your personality matches what other people observe about you:

1. Talk to SOMEONE WHO KNOWS YOU.

"Hey, we've been friends for years. I would totally agree that you are disorganized in every way, but you work so well with others that the job gets done."

2. Talk to SOMEONE WHO EVALUATES YOU.

Definitely outgoing!
Team player!
Follows the rules!
Mrs. Jones, teacher
Coach Kelly
Boss Frank

Verifying Your Responses (continued)

3. Talk to SOMEONE WHO WILL BE HONEST WITH YOU.

"You know that Grandma loves you! You are the smartest, handsomest boy ever! But it would be nice to know that you will show up on time when you say you're going to help me!"

4. Observe YOURSELF OVER TIME:

"Wow, I used to hold a grudge against friends when they would tease me. But now I see that they were just being immature. It doesn't matter to me now. I'm not going to bother being upset anymore."

Name____ Date______________

Worksheet 27

Your Personality Profile

You have thought about your personality traits, rated yourself, and hopefully feel confident about your responses. How can you describe yourself to others with all of this information?

1. Look over your responses about functioning in a GROUP setting. Write a sentence that describes you. For example, "I prefer to work on tasks without other people around."

2. Check over your thoughts about how you ORGANIZE things. Write a sentence. For example, "I like to see the big picture, the big finish, and not worry so much about the details."

3. Now think about how you make DECISIONS. Write a sentence that reflects your personality. For example, "I like to get help and advice from others before making a big decision."

4. Next, focus on your DEMEANOR, or what your personality is mostly like. This might be something like, "I'm pretty quiet but I'm always aware of what's happening with other people."

5. Finally, add something PERSONAL or SPECIAL about yourself. What do people like about the way you are? This could be something such as, "I'm a happy person. People say that being around me makes them feel happy too."

Name____ Date____________

Worksheet 28

Why Personality Matters

Why is it important to know your personality traits? Match the following reasons with the examples.

A. This person can avoid a bad situation by predicting how they will feel or act.

B. This person will enjoy being with people who are similar to them.

C. This person will grow and see new things by being with people who are different from them.

D. This person can show others how to act in situations so we can imitate their behavior.

E. This person can involve themself in situations in which they know they will succeed!

1. "Hey, Mike! I know you don't really like to dance, but a lot of us are going to take a hip hop class for fun. Come join us."

2. "The 3 o'clock movie is going to be filled with lots of young children. If noise and running around bother you, go to the 7 o'clock showing instead."

3. "We need someone who is really creative to help us design the homecoming float. We all want you, Theo! You did an awesome job last year!"

4. "Roberto is going to try to convince his teacher to delay the final exam for a few days. He is a really good persuader. Let's watch him in action!"

5. "Calling all swimmers! We're all going to the lake. Everyone's invited. Just show up. It's going to be a beautiful day, and we can swim all afternoon until it gets dark. Bring sunscreen. Hey, Lucia, I know you love to swim. Will we see you there?"

Name________________________________ Date____________

Worksheet 29

Job/Task Match with Your Personality

Read the personality traits of each person in the following and the job/task requirements. What do you think of the matchups?

1. Zoe is very quiet and prefers to work alone without a lot of people around. She's very creative but slow at making decisions.

   Job: Give tours at the local art gallery.

2. Jimmy is very good at planning things—no detail skips his list. He likes to be the leader in situations.

   Task: Research a vacation spot for three families who want to travel for a week.

3. Adrienne loves to be the center of attention. She rarely asks for advice; she'd rather just make a decision and go with it.

   Task: Join an impromptu comedy sketch group.

4. Liam has a unique way of organizing things—no one else can figure out where anything is.

   Task: Be in charge of a class project in which everyone adds photos or mottos to a hallway bulletin board.

5. Philip resents being criticized and holds a grudge against anyone who has ever said anything unflattering about him.

   Job: Fast-food worker at a very busy restaurant.

Name________________________ Date__________

Worksheet 30

Can You Change Your Personality?

You may not be able to change your entire personality because you are who you are for many reasons; however, you can change some of your behaviors to hone your desirable personality traits. Here are some examples:

1. Learn people-pleasing behaviors. Simple acts such as looking someone in the eye, smiling at them, and using their name in conversation are ways to have people look favorably at you.

2. Become an actor! You may not feel like being outgoing today, but your job requires you to speak first, give information, and pretend that you are excited about what you are doing.

3. Plan ahead and do your research. If you are going to be in a social gathering, find out ahead of time who will be there and what they are interested in. Look up some facts and information about topics that might be discussed. You don't have to fake your knowledge, but you can ask questions that enable others to talk about what they know.

4. Bury old topics or grudges. If you have decided that a grudge or social slight is not worth hanging on to, decide to end the discussion of it. Other good topics to bury are gossiping about other people, endlessly bringing up old stories that no one is interested in, or providing way too many details for another person to listen to.

5. Realize that you have already changed some personality traits just by growing up. Remind yourself of the times when you made better decisions, forgave people faster, showed more leadership than before, and realized whom to go to for advice.

Part II

Learning Basic Social Skills

Introductory Comments

Rationale: We live in a social world. It is important to be able to make judgments as to how best to fit in with the people around us. We need to not only assess ourselves and our personality traits, but now add the element of making judgments as to how we relate to others.

This part of the book is divided into three chapters with many subskills. Chapter 3, "Skills to Make a Good Impression," deals with presenting oneself in a favorable manner. This includes attributes such as having a positive appearance, maintaining personal space, using appropriate language, and developing listening skills.

Chapter 4, "Skills for Self-Improvement," involves developing skills to become a more positive person. This includes developing a good sense of humor, standing up for oneself, making good decisions, and using common sense.

Chapter 5, "Skills for Interacting with Others," delves a little deeper into honing skills that go below the surface of a relationship, such as being able to predict what is expected in a situation, negotiating situations that may be unclear, forming opinions, and being socially accepting of others who may have different outlooks.

Where to Go for More

Making a First Impression
https://teenage.com.sg/campus/9-ways-to-make-a-good-first-impression-2/
(meeting new people and forming friendships)

Being a Better Listener
https://lifeteen.com/blog/10-steps-becoming-better-listener/
(hints for teens to become better listeners)

https://www.lifehack.org/789807/listening-skills
(for all ages)

Developing a Sense of Humor
https://nobelcoaching.com/raising-your-children-with-laughter/
(short article about types of humor)

https://www.edutopia.org/blog/laughter-learning-teens-tough-crowd-matt-bellace
(article for educators specifically about using comedy in the classroom)

Standing Up for Yourself
https://middleearthnj.org/2020/12/07/teaching-teens-to-stand-up-for-themselves-in-the-right-way/
(passive, aggressive, and assertive styles described)

Dealing with Embarrassing Moments
https://www.lifehack.org/597740/the-ultimate-guide-to-dealing-with-every-embarrassing-moment-in-life
(article about general types of embarrassment)

Peer Pressure
https://www.talkitoutnc.org/peer-pressure/types-of-peer-pressure/
(six types of peer pressure common in middle school)

https://kidshealth.org/en/teens/peer-pressure.html
(article for adults about types of peer influence)

Tips for Teachers

Here are some classroom tips to help students learn to make a good impression, enhance self-esteem, and interact with others.

1. *Recognize leadership in students and affirm them by calling attention to positive examples.* "You did an excellent job organizing and completing that class activity. It's nice to know I can count on you." Be honest in your praise—students expect you to be fair with them.
2. *Find pictures of teenagers engaged in common social activities and have students write a word bubble that says what they think each person is saying.* Ask them to explain what clues they used to determine what was being said. Could this apply in any way to what they look like to others?
3. *Play short segments of music or recordings of well-known people (for example, popular singers, actors, commercials with celebrities).* How quickly can the student identify the person by the voice alone? Are there certain voices that they find interesting, annoying, pleasing, or other characteristics? What do they think their own voice conveys to others?
4. *To highlight work ethic in the classroom, start a counting system, such as fifty days without a single lost assignment, seven days without a failed test, nineteen days with perfect attendance, and so on.*
5. *If you have a class newsletter, take turns highlighting a student.* Find out a few mysteries, little-known facts, surprises, and so on about this student. Don't forget pictures!
6. *If you have a class clown, try to use that person to your advantage.* Perhaps they can tell a joke of the day, give a unique perspective on a school event, or prepare a skit for the benefit of the class.
7. *Show that teachers have a sense of humor by putting a joke or cartoon on a test, displaying a bulletin board of baby pictures of teachers (with their permission), or creating a worksheet or drill sheet that has a code that translates to a riddle.* You might put one silly question on a test that students can answer creatively. (Math: If you received $1.50 for every time your little brother or sister annoyed you, how much would you have earned in the past twenty-four hours?)
8. *When possible and appropriate, give your students as much factual feedback on them as you can.* This will give them more information that will help them view themselves realistically. For example: "You got all of the detail questions correct on this reading passage, but you had trouble with sequencing. This is something you need to work on." Or "You tend to start out strong and then you rush at the end of a test and don't read all of the choices carefully. Watch out for that tendency and you'll do better." Give suggestions for improving these areas.
9. *If you have guest speakers visit your classroom, let your students know in advance what your expectations are for being an audience.* If you have a career series of speakers, let your students come up with appropriate questions to ask before the speaker even arrives. This is not a time to ask silly questions or waste the speaker's time.
10. *Discuss what is meant by the "chain of command" and why this is important when being around others.* Why is it better to talk to an immediate supervisor than to try to go directly to the top?
11. *To encourage cooperation, try to avoid situations in which groups are chosen by popularity polls.* Keep groups random and fluid. If a child can't get along with someone in the group, remind them that "the next time" there will be different people to work with.
12. *Demonstrate flexibility within your classroom by having alternative activities for students or backup plans that are known to all.* A fire drill, a snow delay, an unexpected guest speaker, a classroom crisis—any of these events can throw off a tight schedule. Flexibility is a social skill that will get you through many a surprise!

Pointers for Parents

Learning social skills at home is a different type of challenge but can be fun and intentional. Here are some ideas that can be integrated with home activities.

1. *Introduce your child to your friends or acquaintances as the opportunities come up.* Let them observe how you use names, eye contact, and a bit of information to connect people. ("This is my oldest son, Harrison. He's the one who loves to play guitar. Someday we think he'll be a rock star!")
2. *Talk about what was socially appropriate for making a good impression thirty to fifty years ago.* You might want to include grandparents in this activity. Some examples may include the areas of fashion (boys wore suits and ties to a lot more places, girls wore hats and gloves), conversation (women did not talk about certain subjects in mixed groups), and habits (smoking, drinking, and the like).
3. *Prepare your child as much as possible before going into a potentially embarrassing situation.* "Look, I know you don't like to go to the dentist, but getting upset in the waiting room with a lot of people around is not the best time to be angry about it. Let's go over what's probably going to happen, and then talk about how you can best handle it."
4. *Being a good sport about sports (winning or losing) is another opportunity to express to your child the importance of how they appear to others.* "Maybe the umpire needs glasses and the referee is asleep, but it might be a better decision to discuss it at home rather than in public. Sometimes you get a break; sometimes you don't." Life lesson right there.
5. *Have your child evaluate their own performance on a chore or task.* Instead of saying, "You did a pretty good job, but you could have done better on this or that," ask them to tell you how they think they did and explain why, giving details that support this rating.
6. *Children who view themselves as friendless and lonely need extra encouragement.* Ask your child if they would like to have a friend join your family for an event (basketball game, picnic, movie, bowling). Let them pick the person; don't try to force a friendship.
7. *If your child views themself as someone who is always right, proceed with caution and talk about reality.* If they are convinced that they are the best basketball player but can't catch a ball, they will be in for some disappointments when team tryouts come around. Talk about some things that they truly are right about and give evidence for that as well. ("You aren't the best singer, but look at the ribbons you won in 4H for your art! What do you think about that?")
8. *If your child struggles with negative peer pressure, reaffirm your family's values and expectations.* Be clear with your child about what you expect of them in terms of school, leisure time, home responsibilities, and so on. Families have different sets of rules and expectations. It might not be a question of right or wrong but simply the idea that "this is what our family does."
9. *Talk about what types of situations and events affect people differently and how.* Christmas shopping might be stressful, hot days might bring out crabbiness in some, or a holiday coming up might evoke feelings of excitement. How is it helpful to know how these events or situations might affect an individual's being with other people?
10. *Set aside a time for the entire family to tackle a big, needed job around the house, such as painting a bedroom, cleaning out a garage or basement, raking leaves, preparing for company, and so on.* You may find that pitching in together and working as a family can be not only productive but also a lot of fun.

11. *Demonstrate ways to help others feel comfortable when you are out with your child in the community.* Show compassion to an overworked store clerk. Initiate small talk with a waitperson. Return merchandise without being hateful. Your child will see how you handle these seemingly insignificant situations with kindness.
12. *Unfortunately, there are rude people in our daily lives.* A harsh remark, a misunderstanding, or forgetting to put on a turn signal can bring out the worst in people. Teach your child to think big by putting the event in perspective. Will it matter in twenty-four hours? In a year? What is the cost of getting upset? Can you retaliate with creative kindness? How? Raise the atmosphere to a higher level, one person at a time.

Chapter 3

Skills to Make a Good Impression

Skill 6: Making a Good First Impression

INSTRUCTOR PAGES

Rationale: People make judgments about many things based on a first impression. How you look, what you say, how you say it, how you act, and other factors convey a message. Students should be aware of these factors and pay attention to ways they could improve on making a positive first impression.

Worksheet 31: What Is a Good Impression?

Students are to read the paragraphs comparing job applicants and fill in missing words to complete the sentences.

Answer Key:

1. Appearance 2. Habit 3. Friendly, confident, experience 4. Impression

Worksheet 32: Your Appearance

Students are to choose which of two characters appears to be more suited for the activity.

Answer Key:

1. Second 2. Second 3. Second 4. First 5. Second 6. First 7. First 8. Second

Worksheet 33: Your Attitude

Students are to match the attitude conveyed by each character with their comments.

Answer Key:

1. F 2. D 3. A 4. C 5. E 6. B

Question: What are other ways to demonstrate an attitude besides verbal comments?

Worksheet 34: Getting Prepared

Students are to give examples of ways to make a good impression in each situation.

Answer Key: Answers will vary.

Questions: 1. Which of the examples would be more difficult for you? 2. What would you focus on in each example: appearance, attitude, or something else?

Worksheet 35: Asking Appropriate Questions

Students are to discuss why the questions being asked on the worksheet might seem inappropriate.

Answer Key:

1. Bad taste 2. Embarrassing for the other person 3. Too personal 4. Implies that a mistake was made 5. Nosey, not their business 6. Obnoxious

Questions: 1. Can you give other examples of inappropriate questions? 2. Why do you think the characters asked these questions?

Worksheet 36: Pleasantries or Short Conversations

Students are to give examples of a pleasantry in each example.

Answer Key: Answers will vary.

Questions: 1. Why wouldn't you want to have an in-depth conversation in any of these examples? 2. How does a simple gesture or comment make another person feel noticed or important? 3. What are some other examples of ways you might greet someone quickly?

Worksheet 37: Voice Volume and Tone

Students are to identify a problem with a speaker's volume or tone when speaking. The speaker is identified as the character with a * by the image.

Answer Key:

1. A 2. B 3. A 4. A 5. B

Worksheet 38: Using Appropriate Language

Students are to decide which examples show appropriate language in each situation.

Answer Key:

1. Inappropriate (not considerate of sister) 2. Inappropriate (violates school rule) 3. Appropriate (polite) 4. Depends on tone; if teasing, it could be okay; if angry, could show rudeness 5. Inappropriate (probably not clerk's fault) 6. Appropriate (sporting event)

Question: Why is it important to consider where you are or whom you are with when you choose your language?

Worksheet 39: Just Answer the Question!

Students are to pick out the single sentence that answers the question.

Answer Key:

1. "You'll have to turn around and go straight for two miles." 2. "I didn't have time to watch the news." 3. "Here's the $5." 4. "Enormous!"

Question: Why do you think some people find it hard to focus on a simple answer?

Worksheet 40: Introducing Yourself

Students are to decide which characters are introducing themselves in a polite way.

Answer Key:

1. Yes (eye contact, distance) 2. No (slapping on the back) 3. No (no eye contact) 4. Yes (respected no hand shaking) 5. Yes (friendly)

Questions: 1. Which introductions seemed to be the most polite or natural to you? 2. Which situations seemed awkward? Why?

Name____ Date____________

Worksheet 31

What Is a Good Impression?

You are the owner of a jewelry store and need some extra help at the counter. After placing an ad, you receive several phone calls. You are planning to interview several possible workers. You are looking for someone who is friendly, has a nice appearance for an upscale store, and seems to have some experience or at least appears to be a fast learner.

Your first interview is a young man. "Hello," he says to you. "I'm here to apply for the job." You notice his ripped jeans and his T-shirt that says: "I'm Taking Today Off!" There is an odd smell coming from him. You are not sure if it's his greasy hair or if he hasn't had a shower in a while. "Sorry," you hear yourself saying. "I don't think you're quite right for the job." There's just something about the way he looked that you were not impressed by.

Another applicant comes by. At first you are quite interested in the well-groomed girl who comes to your office. Her hair is combed nicely, her clothes are clean and trendy, and—thank goodness—you are sure you smell a whiff of perfume. "Well, so you are here to apply for the job of a clerk," you say to her. "What's your name?" She opens her mouth and does not stop talking for 20 minutes. She has told you her life story, every detail from kindergarten to shopping at the mall yesterday. You are certain that any customer who asked her a question would get much more than they bargained for. You don't like this habit.

Next.

Your next applicant is an older teen. "Good afternoon," he greets you. His smile is friendly, and he appears to be very self-confident. You find out that he has had some experience in sales. He also compliments you on your ruby ring. Now you know he knows something about jewelry! "Are you able to work on weekends?" you ask him. "No problem," he answers. "I'm available whenever you need me." You close the file. "I'll need to check out your references," you say, "but I'm very interested."

What is meant by making a "good impression"?

1. The first applicant for the job didn't care about his ____________.
2. The second applicant looked nice, but she had a very annoying__________.
3. The third applicant appeared to be ______ and very self- _________. He also had some _________ in sales.
4. The third applicant made a good __________ because he seemed to be what the employer was looking for.

Name____ Date______________

Worksheet 32

Your Appearance

Choose which of the following two characters has the better appearance for each situation.

1. Going trick-or-treating

2. Playing football in the mud

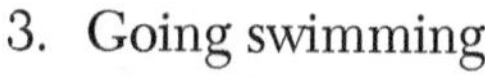

3. Going swimming

4. Going to a formal party

Your Appearance (continued)

5. Riding a horse

6. Taking your dog for a walk in the woods

7. Going for a job interview to mow lawns

8. Going for a job interview to work at a hamburger place

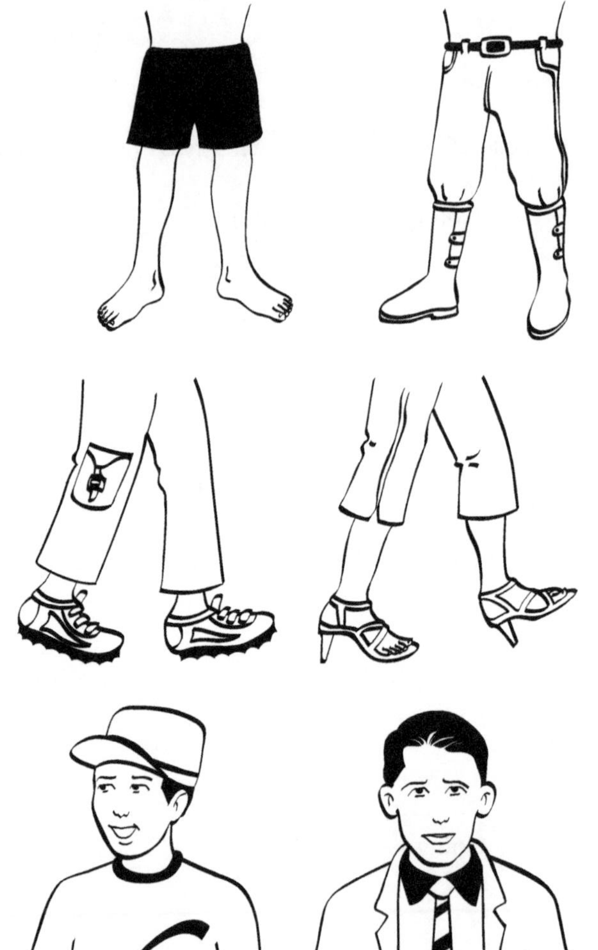

Name____ Date______________

Worksheet 33

Your Attitude

Match the attitude demonstrated in the following by the characters with the impression that it gives.

1. I don't want to talk.
2. I know what I'm doing.
3. I want you to respect me.
4. I'm interested in you.
5. I'm eager to learn.
6. I'm very patient.

a.

When I tell you to do something, you must do what I say, when I say, and how I tell you to do it. Don't question me or what I'm planning—just do it.
COACH

b.

Don't worry if you don't understand this right away; I'll keep explaining until you get it!

c.

Where did you live before you lived here? What do you like to do? Would you like to go with us to the mall?

d.

Watch. You put this CD/DVD in here. Then you push these two buttons. Now wait for the light to go on.

e.

Show me how you drew that! Give me a pencil. May I try?

f.

Yeah. OK. Whatever.

Name____ Date______________

Worksheet 34

Getting Prepared

If you know you need to make a good impression, get yourself ready! What would you need to do to make your best impression in these cases?

1. Talking to the parents of a child you hope to babysit
2. Meeting a cute boy or girl after a game
3. Trying out for the school play
4. Volunteering as a nurse's aide at the hospital
5. Picking up your family's foreign exchange student at the airport
6. Interviewing for a job at the city zoo as an animal caretaker
7. Tutoring elementary students after school
8. Explaining to the track coach why you missed practice
9. Meeting the grandparents of your best friend
10. Trying to get votes to be elected class president

VOTE FOR
ME

Name______________________________ Date__________

Worksheet 35

Asking Appropriate Questions

What is wrong with asking these questions in the following situations?

1.

I heard your dad was sick. Do you think he's going to die?

2.

Hey, your skin looks a whole lot better since you've been going to the skin doctor. Are you still going for treatments?

3.

Did you dye your hair?

Asking Appropriate Questions (continued)

4.
Are you really going to wear those shoes in public?
5.
Was that your mother I saw at the welfare department yesterday? Doesn't she have a job yet?
6.
Where are you going? When will you be back? Is Johnny going with you? May I go too?

Name________________________________ Date____________

Worksheet 36

Pleasantries or Short Conversations

You may encounter short interactions with others in which you are not expected to carry on a full-scale conversation. You can initiate a pleasantry, which is simply giving a polite acknowledgment of the other person (such as a nod or greeting). What are some ways you could be pleasant in the following situations?

1. Getting on a bus and sitting next to someone.

   ____

2. Walking into a theater and having to move over people in the row to get to your seat.

   ____

3. Going up to the busy receptionist in your dentist's office to check in.

   ____

4. Helping to direct people to their seats at a community play.

   ____

5. Showing class visitors where the music rooms are in your school.

   ____

6. Walking down a public street in a thunderstorm and almost running into someone with an umbrella.

   ____

7. Meeting your friend's grandmother at her nursing home.

   ____

8. Letting someone go ahead of you in the checkout line at the store.

   ____

Name____ Date______________

Worksheet 37

Voice Volume and Tone

What is the problem with the volume of the speakers with an asterisk (*) by them in each situation below?

1. __________

Can I help you?
I want a hamburger.
I'm sorry—what did you order?
*

a. Speaker is too soft.

b. Speaker is bored.

2. __________

a. Speaker is angry.

b. Speaker is annoying the person next to him.

GO! GO! YEAH THAT'S THE WAY TO GO !!!!
*

Voice Volume and Tone (continued)

What message is conveyed by the words and tone of each of these people with an asterisk (*) by them? Pick a or b.

3.

Could you pass me that glass?
Like I have nothing better to do.
*

_____ a. You are bothering me.

_____ b. I like to be helpful.

4.

I got an A on my project.
A
Well, aren't you a genius.
*

_____ a. You didn't do that great of a job.

_____ b. You are really smart.

5.

How many times do I have to tell you to put my stuff back where you found it?
*
Sorry!

_____ a. I am concerned about your memory.

_____ b. I am angry at you.

Name____ Date______________

Worksheet 38

Using Appropriate Language

Read the comments and decide which ones are appropriate and which are not. Explain why.

1. Robbie and his friend were taking Robbie's little sister to the park. Robbie wanted to talk about the R-rated movie and know all about what happened in the movie.

2. Sarah got a C− on a test at school and started swearing.

3. Diego and his brother were ordering a pizza at the counter. Diego remembered that he had some coupons from another pizza place and asked the clerk politely if they would be accepted at this restaurant.

4. Juanita had to serve a detention after school for too many tardies to class. She told her friend to wait for her after she got out of prison.

5. David was impatient waiting for the clerk at the drug store to get his prescription. He asked the clerk to please hurry up because he was tired of waiting.

6. Steve and Ramon were cheering for their friends playing a soccer game. They were yelling for them to run faster and score some goals.

Name____ Date____________

Worksheet 39

Just Answer the Question!

Each of these people has been asked a question, but they went way beyond answering the question by giving opinions, getting off-topic, and continuing to talk beyond what the person who asked the question wants to know. Underline the ONE SENTENCE in each conversation that answers the original question.

1.

I'm lost. Can you tell me how to find River Road?

River Road! Boy, you are really off the path. You must have taken a wrong turn about three miles back. I hope you're not in a hurry, because it's a long way back. You'll have to turn around and go straight for two miles.

2.

Did you watch the news last night?
I was so tired when I got home from work! I came home and found something to eat. Then I took a long shower and changed my clothes. I have been putting in a lot of overtime these days. I didn't have time to watch the news. In fact, I didn't have time to watch anything! It's because of all the overtime, you know. I'm just tired all the time.

Just Answer the Question! (continued)

3.

Would you be able to lend me $5?
Why do you always expect me to lend you money? I think you asked for money yesterday, didn't you? Well, you are lucky. Here's the $5. But I'm not going to forget it. And I think you should go get a better job so you don't have to keep borrowing all the time. It wouldn't hurt you to work a little.

4.

What's another word for huge?
Enormous! I can't believe you don't know another word for huge. You sure spend a lot of time doing crossword puzzles. Can I borrow that book when you're done with it? I think it looks like it might be kind of fun.

Name________________________________ Date____________

Worksheet 40

Introducing Yourself

Are these characters introducing themselves to others in a polite way? Pay attention to eye contact, physical contact, distance, and voice!

1.

Nice to meet you, Mr. Martinez. My name is Juan, and I'm a friend of your daughter.

2.

HEY! HOW ARE YOU? You don't mind if I slap you on the back, do you? We're going to be such good friends!

Introducing Yourself (continued)

3.
Uh . . . hello . . .
4.
Nice to meet you. I'd prefer not to shake hands.
No problem! It's very nice to meet you too!
5.
Hi, my name is Florencia. Most people just call me Flo. It's easier!

Skill 7: Being Aware of Your Behavior

INSTRUCTOR PAGES

Rationale: Another way to make a good impression on others is to make sure that your behavior fits in to the setting and situation that you are in. You may not be able to control all of your behaviors, but you can strive to control what you can and not call attention to yourself for behaviors that you can modify.

Worksheet 41: Blending in with a Group

Students are to describe a way that the character could blend in with the crowd that is engaged in an activity.

Answer Key:

1. Enter quietly and join in singing. 2. Enter quietly and find a place to sit. 3. Approach the friends and act interested in participating. 4. Sit at the table with your relatives.

Worksheet 42: Behaviors That You Can't Help

Students are to put a check mark in front of the behaviors that could most likely be controlled or lessened.

Answer Key: Answers may vary.

Questions: 1. Which of the listed behaviors do you think occur because of habit? 2.Which of them might happen because of medical or environmental reasons? 3. What are some ways to reduce unwanted behaviors if you are aware of them happening?

Worksheet 43: Neutral Behavior

When in an unfamiliar situation, a student may want to assume a neutral behavior, that is, hesitate before joining in or making a comment. Students are to indicate which person in each pair is demonstrating a neutral behavior.

Answer Key:

1. Second person—say nothing 2. Second person—pay attention—look, and listen 3. First person—stay back and wait 4. Second person—observe what others are doing first

Questions: 1. Why is waiting for just a few seconds a good way to assess what's going on? 2. What are some situations for which you should NOT wait but get involved quickly?

Worksheet 44: Invading Personal Space

Students are to indicate which characters are invading someone's personal space.

Answer Key: 2, 3, 4

Questions: 1. Why do you think some people prefer greater distance around themselves? 2. How does it make you feel when someone wants to touch you or stand very close to you?

Worksheet 45: Repeating Yourself

Students are to read the examples and discuss whether or not the conversation should be repeated to a new audience.
Answer Key:

1. Annoying 2. OK—requested to repeat story 3. Annoying—led to teasing 4. Annoying—too much detail 5. OK—requested information

Worksheet 46: Being Bossy

Students are to put a check mark by the statements that are bossy rather than helpful.
Answer Key: 1, 2, 4, 5, 7

Questions: 1. Do you think the tone of voice has something to do with sounding bossy? Give an example. 2. Is it being bossy if you are in charge of something and are supposed to assign tasks?

Worksheet 47: Refusing to Be Social

Students are to discuss how the characters in the examples are removing themselves from opportunities to be social.
Answer Key:

1. Avoiding a friendship opportunity 2. Not putting forth effort to volunteer 3. Skipping a birthday party with peers 4. Ignoring a chance to play in a game for fun.

Questions: 1. What opportunities were presented for the characters to participate in a social group? 2. What reasons did the characters give for refusing? 3. What positive outcomes might have happened if the characters agree to join in? 4. Do you think it's a good idea to accept social invitations even if at first they don't sound interesting? Why?

Name______________________________ Date__________

Worksheet 41

Blending in with a Group

If you walked into these situations, what could you do to blend in with the crowd?

Situation 1: Choir class—everyone is singing.

Situation 2: The class is taking a test, and it is very quiet in the room.

Situation 3: Your friends are in the park tossing a football around.

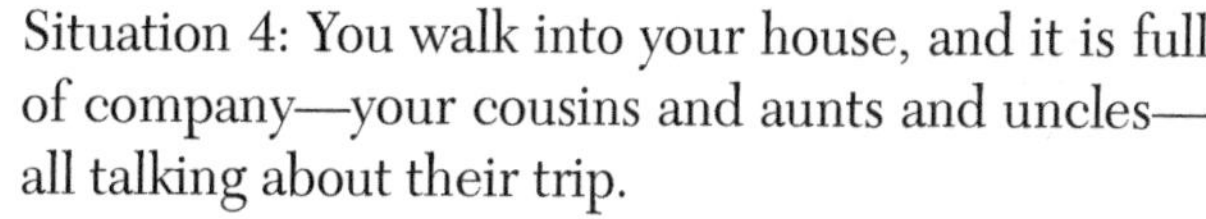

Situation 4: You walk into your house, and it is full of company—your cousins and aunts and uncles—all talking about their trip.

Name____ Date______________

Worksheet 42

Behaviors That You Can't Help

Which of these behaviors can't be controlled easily by a person in most situations? Put a check mark in front of them. Discuss.

___1. Sneezing

___2. Crying

___3. A facial tic

___4. Swearing

___5. Talking loudly

___6. Chewing on your fingernails

___7. Having a seizure

___8. Stuttering

ACHOOOO!

Name____ Date______________

Worksheet 43

Neutral Behavior

When you are in a situation in which you DON'T KNOW WHAT TO DO, which of these behaviors might be the best one to try first?

1. Say something.

Hey !

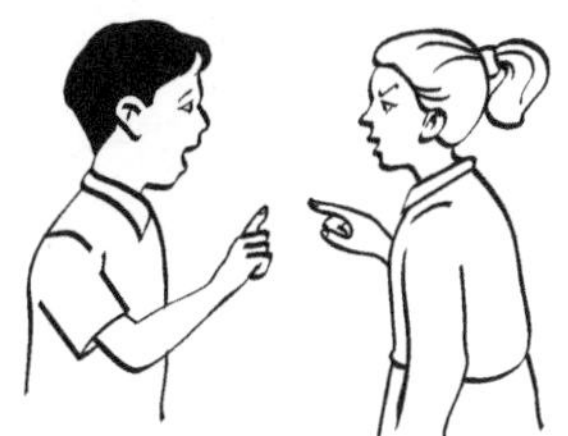

Say nothing.

2. Ask questions about what's going on.

? ?

Pay attention—look and listen.

3. Stay back and wait.

Start telling people what to do.

4. Join in with what others are doing.

Here I come!

Observe what others are doing first and make sure you are welcome.

Name________________________________ Date______________

Worksheet 44

Invading Personal Space

Which of these individuals is showing annoying behavior by invading someone's personal space?

1.

Hi, how are you?
Fine. How are you doing?

2.

Did I ever tell you about my weekend? Well, let me give you ALL the details.

Invading Personal Space (continued)

3.
4.
I'll sit here!
5.
Could you help me with this?

Name____ Date______________

Worksheet 45

Repeating Yourself

Which situations below would be OK for repeating a story? Which would be annoying? Why?

1. Alfonzo told about how his dog got out of the yard and dragged home someone's shoe. Pete came into the room, and Alfonzo told the story again. A few minutes later, Jeff came into the room, and Alfonzo told the story a third time.
2. Mary had a joke about blondes that was really funny. She told the joke to Chantelle, who thought it was great and said that Jennifer would think it was funny, too. When Jennifer came, Mary told the joke to Jennifer. Later, when Brienna came over, Mary told Brienna the joke, too. Everyone thought it was really funny.
3. At breakfast, Pedro accidentally drank some spoiled milk and had to spit it out. His brother, Ricky, thought it was funny, so he told Pedro's friends at school what happened. Later in the day, he told Pedro's teacher what happened. Finally, he told everyone on the bus about Pedro and the milk. Now the kids are teasing Pedro about what he eats.
4. Sofia won a poetry contest and won $100. She told her best friend Karla about it, and Karla was happy for her. The next day, she told Karla every single detail about what her poem was about. Later that day, she reminded Karla that she had $100 because of her poem. Karla didn't seem so happy anymore.
5. Mateo saw a car accident on the way to work. His boss wanted to know what had happened. Later, some friends came up to him and asked what he had seen. By the end of the day, Mateo had told the story about ten times to everyone who was interested.

Name______________________________ Date____________

Worksheet 46

Being Bossy

Some of these statements are bossy, rather than helpful. Put a check mark by the bossy statements.

____ 1. Hand me those papers. Hurry up.

____ 2. We're going to color the map red.

____ 3. Do you have any other ideas for this project?

____ 4. Go get my books.

____ 5. What were you thinking? This poem is terrible. You don't know how to write a poem, obviously.

____ 6. I like the way you used pictures in your report.

____ 7. Angela, you and Teresa did your report all wrong. You aren't going to get a very good grade on it.

____ 8. I have an idea. What do you think about taking turns reading the play?

Name____ Date______________

Worksheet 47

Refusing to Be Social

How are these characters removing themselves from social opportunities?

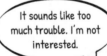

1.

Hey, Colleen, we are going to Shanda's to listen to music. Wanna come?

No, I'm going home to listen to music by myself.

2.

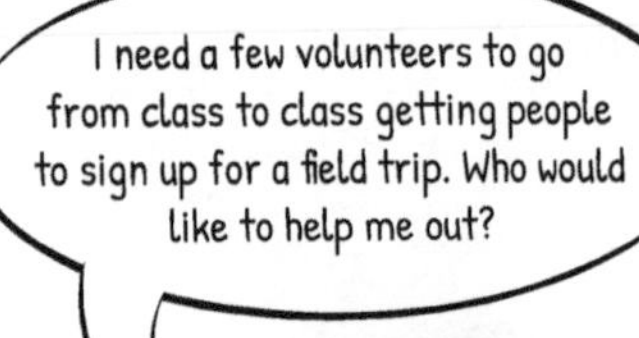
I need a few volunteers to go from class to class getting people to sign up for a field trip. Who would like to help me out?

It sounds like too much trouble. I'm not interested.

Refusing to Be Social (continued)

3.

Oh, here's an invitation to a birthday party. I know most of the girls, but I think I'd rather just read a book.

4.

We are playing some pickup basketball. We could use another player. It's just for fun.
No, some other time maybe.

Skill 8: Being a Good Listener

INSTRUCTOR PAGES

Rationale: Learning to identify good listening skills and then practicing how to listen and remember details are great social skills to work on. It is not always easy to be quiet, to focus on someone else, and to specifically remember details that are important to others.

Worksheet 48: Identifying a Good Listener

Students are to read the skit and answer discussion questions.

Answer Key:

1. Jada 2. She responded to what Christine said, asked questions, gave Christine opportunities to continue to talk. 3. Ignored her comments, changed the subject, left the scene 4. Problems about her sister and grandmother 5. Let her express her feelings, maybe do some problem-solving about the car.

Worksheet 49: How to Be a Good Listener

Students are to match the technique or tip for good listening with the example.

Answer Key:

1. C 2. E 3. A 4. F 5. B 6. D

Questions: 1. Which listening tip do you think you would like to try? 2. How could you practice these specific tips?

Worksheet 50: Important Listening Situations

Students are to explain why a listening situation is important and give a tip that would help.

Answer Key:

1. Need to know the information; repeat the steps back. 2. Need to know for safety reasons; don't interrupt while he is explaining. 3. You are given responsibility; give full attention to your neighbor. 4. You need to use the product properly; repeat the directions. 5. You need to be ready to catch the ball; be very sure of the number. 6. You need to get all of the information you can to help him make a decision; ask questions.

Questions: 1. What's the worst that could happen in the situations if someone didn't listen carefully? 2. Do you have any examples of mistakes that were the result of not listening?

Worksheet 51: What Problems Do You See?

Students are to identify the problem with the listener in each example.

Answer Key:

1. Thinking of something else 2. No eye contact for a visual demonstration 3. Doing something else 4. Did not listen to directions when given 5. Excited about the task, will probably not remember about the lights 6. Did not focus on the friend's concern, gave a flippant comment

Questions: 1. In each case, what could the listener have done better? 2. What could the listener have said to show the other person that they were listening?

Worksheet 52: Remembering Things About Others

Students are to identify if the character on the left is showing that they were listening to the speaker by remembering a detail.

Answer Key:

1. No 2. Yes—boy remembered the cousin liked to bike 3. Yes—boy remembered the girl's birthday 4. Yes—the girl knew exactly what kind of pizza the other girl liked

Questions: 1. What are some ways you could help yourself remember something important about another person? 2. Have you had an experience in which someone remembered a detail about you? How did it make you feel?

Name____ Date______________

Worksheet 48

Identifying a Good Listener

Skit

Characters: Jada, Beth, and Christine—three friends

Setting: Walking down the hallway at school

Task: Identify the good listener.

JADA: Hey, Christine, what's up?

BETH: Yeah, we haven't seen you around for a while. Where are you hiding out?

CHRISTINE (*sadly*): Oh, well, you know I've been having some trouble with my sister. We have to share a room since my old, sick grandmother came to live with us. I lost my private bedroom—not that it was all that great anyway. But now I have to look at my sister all the time.

JADA (*sympathetically*): Hey, that sounds like a real drag.

CHRISTINE: It is; in fact—

BETH: I can't stand my sister. I'll be so glad when she's off to college and I get the whole closet and her CAR! *(starts to cheer)*

JADA (*concerned*): Is your grandmother pretty sick?

CHRISTINE: Yeah, she had a heart attack and was in the hospital.

BETH: My dad's always saying that he's going to have a heart attack one of these days if he doesn't quit smoking. *(pauses)* Do either of you have a cigarette?

JADA: Beth! I thought you quit! *(turns back to Christine)* Will you be going to the game with us on Friday?

CHRISTINE: I'd like to, but it depends on if my dear sister needs the car.

BETH (*suddenly interested*): So you might not be able to drive?

CHRISTINE: Well, I don't know . . . my grandmother is—

BETH: Oh look! There's Paulina! Let's see what she's up to! Come on! *(takes Jada by the arm and pulls her away)*

Identifying a Good Listener (continued)

Discussion Questions

1. Who was the good listener?
2. Why?
3. How could you tell that Beth wasn't interested in listening to Christine?
4. What was on Christine's mind?
5. How could Jada's listening have helped Christine?

Name____ Date______________

Worksheet 49

How to Be a Good Listener

Match the technique or tip on the left with an example on the right that shows a way to be a good listener. Be sure to look at the tips on both pages before you choose.

___1. Use eye contact.

a.

My dad is driving me crazy!
Really? What's happening?

___2. Make comments about the conversation.

b.

I just got back from skiing!
I ski too— but I won't talk about that right now.

___3. Ask questions.

c.

Hi—got a second?
Sure.

How to Be a Good Listener (continued)

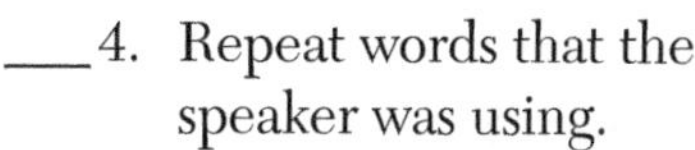

___4. Repeat words that the speaker was using.

d.

And then she said—
I'll stop thinking about the candy bar.

___5. Don't interrupt.

e.

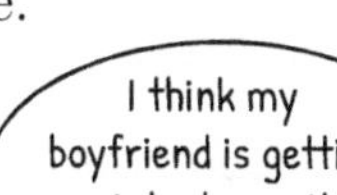

I think my boyfriend is getting into drugs. It scares me.
I can tell you're bothered.

___6. Give your full attention to the speaker.

f.

I'm really worried about my math grade. I'm not sure what to do.
Math grades can be tough!

Name____ Date______________

Worksheet 50

338
x 4

Important Listening Situations

Why is it important to be a good listener in the following situations? What tips or techniques could help you be a good listener?

1. The teacher is explaining a shortcut to solving some multiplication problems.

Why important ______________________________

Listening tips ______________________________

2. Your boss is demonstrating how to operate a new machine for frying French fries.

Why important ______________________________

Listening tips ______________________________

3. Your neighbor is going on vacation to Florida for two weeks and wants you to take care of his horses and chickens.

Why important ______________________________

Listening tips ______________________________

4. Spot has fleas! Your veterinarian is recommending a new product that will take care of the problem if you follow the directions carefully.

Why important ______________________________

Listening tips ______________________________

5. The football coach wants the ball thrown to *you* sometime during the game. The quarterback will call a special number that lets you know it's that play.

Why important ______________________________

Listening tips ______________________________

6. Your best friend is thinking about buying an old car that seems to be running pretty well, but he's not sure it's worth very much. He wants to know what you think.

Why important ______________________________

Listening tips ______________________________

Name____ Date____________

Worksheet 51

What Problems Do You See?

Why is the listener in each situation not doing a very good job? How could they improve their listening skill?

1.

2.

3.

I want you to pick up a pound of hamburger, three bags of chips, and onion buns. Don't get the regular buns!
Yeah, yeah.
Watch carefully. I'll go through this step-by-step so you'll know how to operate this microscope.
Don't forget to be home at 7:00. It's a school night!
Does this piece fit here?

What Problems Do You See? (continued)

4.
I thought you'd never get here! Didn't you turn right after the railroad tracks?
Turn right? Right? What railroad tracks?
5.
Whatever you do, don't turn on the brights. They won't shut off.
I'm so excited about driving your car! Give me the keys!!
6.
I got the worst haircut of my life at the mall. They over-charged me, too!
Do you like my new jeans? I got them at the mall. Oh, your hair's so cute!

Worksheet 52

Remembering Things About Others

One way to show that you are a good listener is by remembering something that a person has mentioned to you. This shows that what they said or did was important to you. In the examples below, is the person on the left showing that they were observant?

1.

2.

Hi, Felicia. Is this the weekend that you are going with your father to New York?
No, it's in three weeks. I've told you that at least four times.
What a good picture of your cousins on Instagram. Is this one the cousin who rode his bike across Wisconsin one summer? Was his name Tony?
Yes, wow, what a good memory! How did you remember that?

Remembering Things About Others (continued)

3.
Happy birthday!
That just made my day!
4.
We would like a large pizza, but no mushrooms and no onions. My friend here does not like much of anything on her pizza! She'll also have iced tea, no ice, one lemon.

Chapter 4

Skills for Self-Improvement

Skill 9: Having a Good Sense of Humor

INSTRUCTOR PAGE

Rationale: What is a greater social skill than having a good sense of humor? Someone who can see an amusing side of situations possesses a very important life skill. Someone who can learn to lighten up and find humor in events has truly taken a big step toward getting along with others, especially in situations in which others are not sure how to react. Someone with a sense of humor can make a hard task fun and a dull day interesting; such a person can help determine others' reactions to what's going on.

Worksheet 53: Benefits of a Sense of Humor

Students are to read the paragraphs describing how a good sense of humor can affect others and are to fill in the blanks in summary sentences.

Answer Key:

1. lighter 2. laugh 3. fun

Worksheet 54: Creating Humor Appropriately

Situations are listed that could have humorous overtones. Students are to think of ways in which these common situations could be funny.

Answer Key: Answers will vary.

Worksheet 55: Easing Tension with Humor

Students are to consider the situations on the worksheet that may have an element of tension about them. They are to think of ways in which humor could help relieve the tension.

Answer Key: Answers will vary.

Worksheet 56: Laughing WITH, not Laughing AT

Students are to indicate which students on the worksheet are laughing *with* other students and which students are laughing *at* other students.

Answer Key:

1. laughing with 2. laughing at 3. laughing at 4. laughing with 5. laughing with 6. laughing with

Worksheet 57: Using Humor to Include Others

Students are to think of ways that others can be included by using humor or humorous situations.

Answer Key: Answers will vary.

Name____ Date______________

Worksheet 53

Benefits of a Sense of Humor

Question: What would you do if you just discovered that you had been walking around for two hours at the mall with a white sock (straight out of the dryer) stuck on the back of your black shirt?

A. Take the sock off quietly and throw it away.

B. Be embarrassed and ask a friend if anybody saw it.

C. Laugh and say, "Hey, where's the other one?"

If you picked (C), chances are you may have a good sense of humor. Having a good sense of humor means that you are able to see or find the lighter side of a situation.

A person with a good sense of humor might create humor in situations by being playful, saying funny comments that make others laugh, and not being afraid to laugh at himself or herself. A person with a good sense of humor might see a person with a broken leg and say, "Well! Some people will do anything to get out of gym." This might make the person with the broken leg feel better.

A person with a good sense of humor can laugh at himself or herself and even poke fun at their situation. The sock on the back of a shirt is seen as not a big deal—it's funny! The person might be embarrassed but won't let others know or be embarrassed for him or her.

People with a good sense of humor are fun to be around. They might be the class clown, causing others to laugh. Of course, even the class clown has to know when it is the right time to laugh and when to be quiet. Parties are more fun with these people around. Even if you aren't one of the people who makes others laugh, if you are one who joins in the fun and laughter, you will show that you have a good sense of humor, too.

1. A person with a good sense of humor is able to see or find the ______________ side of a situation.
2. A person with a good sense of humor can ____________________ at himself or herself.
3. People with a good sense of humor are ____________________ to be around.

Name ________________________________ Date ____________

Worksheet 54

Creating Humor Appropriately

What could be humorous about the following situations? Make a cartoon, role-play with others, or talk about how something could be funny without being rude or hurtful.

1. School lunches ____________________
2. Shopping with parents ____________________
3. Getting a haircut ____________________
4. Excuses for not having homework done ____________________
5. Odd relatives ____________________
6. Being late ____________________
7. Going to the dentist ____________________
8. Exercising ____________________
9. Waiting in a long line ____________________
10. Walking the dog ____________________

Who's walking who?

Name______________________________ Date__________

Worksheet 55

Easing Tension with Humor

How could having a good sense of humor ease the tension in these situations? How could it help someone feel less embarrassed or feel included in a group?

1. You are late for your friend's surprise birthday party. When you walk in, everyone is glaring at you because you might just spoil the surprise!
2. You thought it was dress-up day at school and wore your Sunday best—while everyone else is in jeans and T-shirts.
3. Your two best friends are angry at each other and put you in the middle. Both show up at the hamburger place expecting to eat with you.
4. Your dog ran in the muddy yard and snuck into the house—all over your mother's clean kitchen floor. To make matters worse, your company (mother's boss) is coming up the driveway now!
5. You lent some jeans to your friend and they accidentally got red paint all over them. They feel terrible! You do too, but it's not worth getting all upset about it.
6. Your cousins are visiting and you took a lot of pictures of your group swimming in the lake. The one that they chose to post on Facebook is great of them but terrible of you! Before you can stop them, it's posted. You are trying to think of a clever comment to make.
7. What a klutz! You are walking through the cafeteria, past the table where the popular people sit, and trip!!! Your lunch is all over the floor!!!
8. Your science study group worked long and hard on the science fair project—only to have someone's little sister knock it over and break it into pieces. No one is laughing.

Name____ Date______________

Worksheet 56

Laughing WITH, not Laughing AT

Which of the cartoons show characters who are laughing WITH others in a situation? Which show characters who are laughing AT others? Circle either WITH or AT.

1.

Oh Look! We both must have gone to the same store!
With At

2.

Look at that project! Did first graders do that? Ha ha!
With At

3.

Did she say 5 times 5 is 50? Where'd she come up with THAT?
With At

4.

Whoops! Sorry! Thanks for blocking my fall on this slippery floor!
With At

Laughing WITH, not Laughing AT (continued)

5.

Oh, look at how funny we looked! Look at our clothes! And our hair!!!
PHOTO ALBUM

With At

6.

I know, I know...this dress is ridiculous. But it's my sister's wedding and she gets to pick what we look like! I'll get her back when I get married!

With At

Name____ Date______________

Worksheet 57

Using Humor to Include Others

Here are some examples of ways that others can be included by using humor. Can you think of other ways? Draw or write your own.

1.
Want to sign this card for Barry? His birthday is tomorrow and we're going to surprise him.
HAPPY BIRTHDAY
3.
Come on in — the water's fine for all of us little whales!
5.
Sandra's really embarrassed about her new haircut. Let's all separately ask her where she got it cut and say we want one just like it!

2.
Ha, ha, ha, ha, ha! Hey, read this!
4.
You look like someone who needs chocolate!
6.
It was really funny when Tom made a basket for the other team! We won anyway, but let's call him "Sharpshooter" when we see him!

Skill 10: Communicating

INSTRUCTOR PAGES

Rationale: There are many ways to communicate these days: email, text messaging, instant/direct messaging, cell phone, voice mail, and probably even others. But if the message is not received, or not received with the original intent, it is still a lost message. We also need to be aware of the benefits of waiting before responding (because new information can change the whole situation) and of knowing when a conversation should be between only two people rather than a busload of people who have to listen to a private conversation on a cell phone. These are all ways of expressing ourselves, but we still need to make sure messages are sent, received, and understood.

Worksheet 58: Expressing Yourself with Words

Characters on this worksheet have something that they need to express verbally. Students are to suggest what each character could say.
Answer Key: Answers may vary.

1. "Mrs. Brown, I think there might be a mistake on this. Could you check it for me?"
2. "Hi, this is the wrong game. What is the policy for exchanging it?"
3. "Hi, Jeri—am I on time?"
4. "Coach, could you tell me again?"

Worksheet 59: Waiting Before Responding

Sometimes even a moment or two of thinking can prevent words or actions that you will later regret. In each situation, students are to write down their first reaction to the situation. Then, with additional information, students are to write down their second (and, we hope, better) response.
Answer Key: Answers may vary.

1. "I'M NOT LATE!!"; "I thought I was on time. Thanks for telling me about the clock."
2. "I can't believe I got Cs! Those teachers are so mean!"; "Oh, I'm glad I made that mistake! Poor Angelica!"
3. "Hey! Quit pushing me, you bully!"; "No problem. (My arm will heal in six weeks—ha ha.)"

Worksheet 60: Avoiding Getting Upset

Some people know exactly what button to push to get you upset. Maybe it is a teasing phrase, a look, or reminding you of a mistake. Students are to write down one way that the person on the worksheet could communicate how they feel.
Answer Key (Examples):

1. Ignore the little brother; walk away.
2. Get a lock for the toolbox; make a sign "Ask First!"

3. Plan on having a few phrases ready to say to the aunt; have a serious discussion with her if that is appropriate.
4. Ask if he can talk to the teacher in private.
5. Talk honestly with Karla about how this bothers her.

Worksheet 61: Public Versus Private Conversations

Which discussions on the worksheet are probably best kept private? Students are to mark the examples as Public or Private.

Note: You can add more topics, appropriate to your students' age, grade, problems, and so on.

Answer Key:

1. public 2. public 3. private 4. public 5. private (may be annoying to others) 6. private 7. private if the intent is to give away answers to those who have not yet taken the test 8. private (not everyone may want to hear the details, and your mother may not want you discussing this either)

Worksheet 62: Controlling Your Feelings

Sometimes what you feel and what you communicate or feel can be two different things. Students are to discuss what each character really feels and then what they actually communicate to others.

Answer Key (answers may vary):

1. Feels sad; communicates hope 2. Is unhappy with the gift; communicates thankfulness 3. Feels that he did an adequate job; communicates cooperation 4. Feels joy; communicates toned-down enthusiasm 5. Feels unsure of himself; communicates initiative to join in

Name________________________________ Date____________

Worksheet 58

Expressing Yourself with Words

These students need to say something in order to be understood. What do you think each could say?

Situation 1 ____

Tabitha thinks her teacher Mrs. Brown made a mistake on her math test. She is upset because the grade she gets will go on her report card.

D

Situation 2 ____

Tom got the wrong game for his brother's birthday present. He wants to return it to the store.

GAME

Expressing Yourself with Words (continued)

Situation 3 ____

Elinore is very hurt because her best friend didn't save a place for her at the restaurant. She doesn't understand why.

Situation 4 ____

Paul's soccer coach told him what to do when he goes back into the game. Paul isn't sure he understands what he is supposed to do.

COACH
10

Name________________________________ Date__________

Worksheet 59

Waiting Before Responding

Sometimes it is better to wait before speaking. Write down your first response after reading the first part of the situation. Write a better response after you read the second part.

Situation 1

Peter arrived at work on time, or at least he thought he was on time. When he got to the time clock, it showed that he was ten minutes late. His boss walked up to him and said, "Looks like you're late, Peter."

1st response: ____

Then the boss said, "We've been having trouble with that machine. I know you were on time."

2nd response: ____

Waiting Before Responding (continued)

Situation 2
Angela picked up her report card and saw that she had Cs in every subject. She was angry that her teachers gave her Cs when she KNEW that she had done well.

1st response: ______________________________

She looked again and saw that she had picked up a report card that said "Angelica" on it, not "Angela."

2nd response: ______________________________

Situation 3
Jorge was accidentally pushed in the hallway by one of the bigger, older students.

1st response: ______________________________

The big guy apologized to Jorge, saying that he was late to class and didn't see him.

2nd response: ______________________________

Name____ Date______________

Worksheet 60

Avoiding Getting Upset

Each person knows how they will probably respond to certain situations that will get them into trouble. Write down one way that the person could communicate how they feel.

1. Allie hates being called "Al." She knows that her little brother loves to tease her in front of her friends.

   ____

   ____

2. Juan gets upset when people mess with his things. At work, someone borrowed his tools and didn't replace them.

   ____

   ____

3. Lucinda has gained a few pounds. Her aunt, who always talks about weight, is coming to visit for the weekend.

   ____

   ____

4. Derek has not had much sleep in the past few days because of family problems. He has a big test coming up, and he hasn't studied for it. He knows the teacher is going to give him a lecture about studying more.

   ____

   ____

5. Denise can't stand it when her friend Karla always tries to take over the conversation when there are boys around. She wants to be friends with Karla, but this really bothers her.

   ____

   ____

Name ______________________________ Date ______________

Worksheet 61

Public Versus Private Conversations

Which of these conversations should be private, rather than held with other people around? Mark the items as Private or Public.

__________ 1. Talking about studying for a test

__________ 2. Talking about how you hate rainy days

__________ 3. Talking about how your father hurt your feelings

__________ 4. Talking about a TV show that you like

__________ 5. Talking on a cell phone about how angry you are at your sister

__________ 6. Laughing loudly at the clothes on the lady in front of you on the bus

__________ 7. Talking about the correct answers on a test

__________ 8. Explaining your mother's surgery in great detail

Other private topics:

____

____

Name____ Date______________

Worksheet 62

Controlling Your Feelings

The following characters have some very strong feelings about what happened to them. But what they show is different from what they feel. Try to identify both emotions in each case. Why is the second one more socially acceptable?

What Happened | **What They Feel** | **What They Show**

1. Sebastian didn't make the football team, even though he practiced all summer, every day.

I can't believe
I tried so hard and
I didn't make it!

Maybe I'll try
out next season.

2. Serenity got a birthday gift: a perfectly horrid pin from Great Aunt Stella.

YUCK!
Thank you—
it's very...
unique!

3. Jayden's boss was in a BAD mood. Nothing Jayden did was right. Finally the boss yelled at him and told him to do the dishes over.

These dishes
are FINE!

OK. No
problem.

4. Aaliyah got an A+ on a difficult test in English. Her best friend (also her study buddy) got a D.

YES!!

I did OK.

5. Nathan moved to a new school district where he is one of a few minority students.

Will they
like me?

Hi—may I
join you?

Skill 11: Standing Up for Yourself

INSTRUCTOR PAGE

Rationale: It is important to view yourself as someone who is strong enough to stand up for yourself and for your beliefs. This does not mean you are always right, of course, but if you truly believe in something, live like it. It takes courage to go against the crowd, but others will respect someone who is not afraid to stand up for themself.

Worksheet 63: That's Not Right!

This worksheet has a short story about a boy who stands up to two bullies on behalf of a weaker boy. Students are to respond to questions after reading the story.

Answers may vary.

Answer Key:

1. Belief that big people shouldn't pick on little people 2. Two bullies 3. I like him. 4. Yes 5. There might be a fight or it might end peacefully.

Worksheet 64: Why Do You Think That Way?

Students may have strong beliefs for certain reasons. On this worksheet, students are to match the character who has a strong belief with the probable reason WHY they feel so strongly. How can this relate to their own strong beliefs?

Answer Key:

1. A (father's experience) 2. D (values education) 3. B (experience of not being repaid) 4. C (taught by family) 5. E (logical)?

Worksheet 65: What's the Problem?

The characters on this worksheet believe something strongly, but some of them are not on the right track. Students are to pick out the characters who have a shaky basis for their beliefs and discuss why.

Answer Key:

1. *Boy A* believes it's OK for him to go to an R-rated movie; *Boy B* believes he shouldn't go if his parents wouldn't allow him to.
2. *Girl A* believes that her grandmother will embarrass her; *Girl B* believes that her uncle may be different, but that's not a problem.
3. *Boy A* believes that his best effort is good enough; *Boy B* believes that copying the answers is the way to get a good grade.
4. *Girl A* believes it is OK to lie about merchandise that has been used; *Girl B* believes that is not all right.
5. *Boy A* believes that Lin always wins the spelling bee; *Boy B* believes it is because her parents are rich; *Girl C* believes it is because girls are smarter than boys; *Boy D* believes she won because of her effort; and *Boy E* believes she won because of racial characteristics.

Name____ Date______________

Worksheet 63

That's Not Right!

Read the story about Tomas. Try to determine what is important to him and how he shows that.

Tomas walked into gym class and was getting ready to play basketball when he noticed Jon and Alberto, two rather large boys, teasing Frank, the class nerd. This time, Jon was dangling Frank's glasses just out of his reach as the small boy desperately tried to grab them. "Jump higher, Pee Wee," Jon teased.

Tomas put his hands on his hips and shook his head. Frank was indeed an easy target. He wore thick glasses, had a speech problem, and was very small for his age. On top of that, he would rather work on a computer than catch a basketball any day.

"Why don't you knock it off and leave him alone," Tomas demanded, stepping up to the now-increasing circle of students.

"Why don't you stay out of this?" advised Alberto, shaking a finger in Tomas's face. He gave Frank a shove, knocking him to the ground.

Tomas turned to the rest of the class, who were watching with increasing interest. No one seemed to want to get too involved. "So how many of you are tired of watching these bullies harass other people?" he demanded of his audience. "Who's ready to say with me that this isn't right; enough is enough?"

At first there was a silence that seemed to last forever. Then one by one, hands went up. The two bullies looked at the vote that was taken by their peers. Every hand was up.

That's Not Right! (continued)

"You might be able to take care of one small boy," Tomas said to the bullies. "You might even be able to put me down, too. But you better think carefully before you take on ALL of us."

1. What belief did Tomas stand up for?
2. Who did he stand up to?
3. How do you feel about Tomas?
4. Would you like Tomas for a friend?
5. What might happen next?

Name________________________________ Date____________

Worksheet 64

Why Do You Think That Way?

People have various reasons for their beliefs. Match each comment by the person on the left with the REASON why that person believes it on the right.

1. My father was an alcoholic. I remember watching him abuse my mother and other family members. Then I watched him slowly die as his liver gave out. I will never take even one drink.
2. To have lots of choices in what you do with your life, I think it's important to get a college education.
3. Sorry, I'm not going to lend you any money. The last two times I did, you never paid me back. Your excuses didn't make any sense. Sorry.
4. We were taught to pray before meals. We have always done it, we will always do it, and when I have a family of my own, you can bet that we'll still be doing it!
5. If you take good care of your car, it will last a lot longer. Just read the maintenance manual!

a. Experience of someone you know
b. Your own experience
c. Taught by someone else
d. Something you value
e. Something that sounds logical or makes sense if you think about it

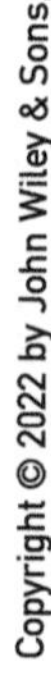

Name________________________________ Date______________

Worksheet 65

What's the Problem?

The characters are standing up for what they believe, but what problem(s) do you see with what some of them believe?

1.
Hey, I know this movie is rated "R," but Joey's dad will take us. Let's go!
a.
My parents don't want me to go to "R" movies. I'll join you guys later.
b.
2.
I want to have some of the kids from school come over, but my grandmother only speaks German and I'm afraid she'll embarrass me.
a.
My uncle from Puerto Rico is staying for a few days. He's got some interesting stories to tell. Come on over; you'll enjoy him!
b.
3.
This test is really hard. But I'll do my very best.
a.
Johnny has the answers to the test! If you copy them down, you'll get an A!!!
b.
4.
Let's get these jeans, wear them to the party, and then take them back and say they were the wrong size. That way we won't have to pay for them.
a.
That's not right. I'm not going to be a part of that!
b.
5.
Lin won the spelling bee again this year. You know she always wins.
a.
She won because her parents are rich.
b.
She won because girls are smarter than boys.
c.
She won because she studies the words and knows how to spell them.
d.
NO, she won because Asians are smarter than other races.
e.

Skill 12: Making Good Decisions

INSTRUCTOR PAGES

Rationale: Making decisions usually involves other people. When we make good decisions, they can affect other people in a positive way. Making poor decisions can cause harm and pain to others (for example, parents, children, and family members). It is often difficult to make decisions, especially when a lot is at stake. However, by having and using a commonsense strategy for making decisions, we may be able to clarify what is important to everyone involved.

Worksheet 66: Questions to Ask Yourself

This worksheet details some questions that can be helpful in narrowing down what information is important to make a good decision. Students are to read the information and answer the accompanying questions.

Answer Key:

1. minor or trivial 2. decision 3. reversed 4. urgent, time 5. guides, relationship

Worksheet 67: A Decision-Making Chart

This chart shows some logical steps involved in making decisions. Questions that can lead to eliminating some options or the realization that more information is needed help guide the learner through a process for making decisions. Students will think of a decision they have coming up and walk through the steps on the chart.

Answer Key: Answers will vary.

Worksheet 68: What Decision Needs to Be Made?

Students are to select the most obvious decision that needs to be made in the situations listed on the worksheet. Then, by using the decision-making chart (worksheet 67) and its questions, students can go through the process of making a good decision appropriate for the situation.

Answers may vary.

Answer Key:

1. Deciding what treatment is most appropriate for the dog: Putting her down? Trying more medication?
2. Deciding what treatment is most appropriate for Grandma: Should she go to a nursing home? Have a visiting nurse? Receive more or different medication?
3. Deciding what you will do after high school: Work? Vocational training? College?
4. Deciding whether or not to buy the house; more information is needed about the cost, payments, and so on.
5. Janelle needs to decide whether or not marriage is truly the best option for her.
6. Deciding when to take the vacation.
7. Deciding how quickly you can get medical treatment.
8. Deciding whether to call the police or check out the noise.
9. Deciding what to do about feeding everybody.
10. Deciding whether or not to go to school, take the test, ask for more time, and so on.

Questions: 1. What are some decisions you have had to make recently? 2. What factors helped you make your decision?

Worksheet 69: When You Need More Information

In each case, further information is needed to help make a good decision. Students are to come up with examples of the type of information that is necessary or helpful.

Answers may vary.

Answer Key:

1. How secure his present job is; if he can afford the payments (plus the insurance)
2. The difference in price between the flights; how much time is spent waiting for (and between) planes
3. What kind of computer you can afford; what options and programs you may need
4. What kind of person Mark is; what Mark looks like; Mark's interests
5. How much time is involved in each sport; whether you are more skilled at one than at the other
6. If you plan to need history credits for college; other opinions about Mr. Peters as a teacher
7. How much the insurance costs; how you will obtain the money
8. What you have to do to earn the money; if you have to put money up-front before you get paid; if this is a legitimate business proposition

Worksheet 70: Head Versus Heart Decisions

Some decisions that work out well can be made impulsively or "by instinct"; however, using common sense might better steer you toward a good decision. Students are to consider possible problems with the impulsive decisions on the worksheet.

Answers may vary.

Answer Key:

1. The shares of stock may lose value.
2. Later, the girl may decide that a secure person would have made her life easier.
3. The puppy is against the rules, will probably bark and get her into trouble, and will outgrow the size of the small apartment.
4. The person will end up paying a lot of extra money on interest charges.
5. The person may not want to put forth the extra work to become a doctor, but later may wish that she could help children's medical needs; also the difference in pay may later be a consideration.
6. The girl may wish she had gotten some money for the tickets.

Questions: 1. Do you think of yourself as an impulsive decision-maker or do you think things over? 2. Can you give an example of an impulsive decision that turned out very well?

Worksheet 71: Not Everything Is a Crisis

The student is to match a possible solution with a situation that seems like a disaster to the character. There may be more than one good solution.

Answer Key:

1. A, B, D 2. A, D 3. B 4. D 5. A, B

Questions: 1. Do you think these situations would be a crisis for most people or could they just be particularly annoying to an individual? 2. What strategy do you choose when you are feeling panicked or upset about something going wrong?

Worksheet 72: What Is Common Sense?

Students are to read the paragraphs about common sense and fill in the blanks.
Answer Key:

1. sense 2. knowledge; resourceful 3. clues or answers 4. harder 5. common sense

Worksheet 73: Looking for Clues

Charlie is a character with little common sense. Students are to look at the pictures and figure out how Charlie could easily answer his own questions without bothering anyone else.
Answer Key:

1. look at the calendar 2. look at the directory 3. read the note—books are not needed 4. look at the rain outside 5. use the GPS on your phone 6. check to see if the TV is plugged in

Questions: 1. What are some commonsense questions that you could ask right now in your present situation? 2. What clues are around you to help answer the questions?

Worksheet 74: Using Your Common Sense

Each situation on this worksheet portrays a character who is not using common sense or who is in a situation in which they need to do something that requires common sense. Students are to make suggestions.

Answers may vary.
Answer Key:

1. Pay the book rental; there will be other sales.
2. Wait until after the move to start such a big project.
3. Magic markers don't erase; David needs to use a pencil.
4. Justine should get her cat spayed and work hard to find good homes for the kittens.
5. They should take water bottles and sunscreen with them.
6. Carmine needs to practice more, not just before his lesson.
7. Antonio needs to use sunscreen or stay in the shade.
8. Kara could call her mother at home to bring her running shoes.

Questions: 1. Can you think of other examples of using common sense in your daily activities? 2. Do you think that you possess and use common sense often? Give examples.

Name____ Date______________

Worksheet 66

Questions to Ask Yourself

Think of all the decisions you make in a day! Will you have cereal or donuts for breakfast? Will you have time for breakfast at all? Should you wear black jeans or blue? Get to class early or hang out in the hall in hopes of accidentally-on-purpose running into someone special? Go to a movie or clean your room? (Well . . . some decisions are more obvious than others!) Throughout the day you are faced with lots of decisions to make.

?
Cheeries
DoNuts

Here are some questions to ask yourself that might make it easier to come to a decision:

- **How important is this decision?** Some decisions are relatively minor and don't make a lot of difference. The color of your clothes or what movie you see may not have a long-term impact on your life past that day. However, other decisions are very important and can affect the course of your life. Decisions affecting what you'll be doing after high school, choosing a college or vocation, getting a job, getting married, deciding where you'll live, whether or not to buy a house, having children and . . . wow! It never stops!
- **How does your decision affect others?** If you break up with Wally, are all of his friends going to snub you? If you go against your parents' wishes because you don't want to go to law school, will they cut you out of the will? If you join one group, does that exclude joining another group? If you decide you're not going to drive your friends to Florida over spring break (and you're the one with the car), how will that affect your relationship with your friends? And what if you decide to give the $10,000 from Aunt Jane to the local animal shelter in memory of Buffy the kitty instead of going to college—how will that affect Aunt Jane?
- **Is the decision reversible?** If you choose one path—for example, going to the community college and working for a year instead of borrowing the money to go to an Ivy League school—could you still end up at your goal of completing college? You may be able to take a risk if you have a good backup plan. But first think through the consequences. Can you live with your choice if you're stuck with it?
- **How urgent is the decision?** Do you have to make a life-and-death call right now? Call 911? Buy the car while it's on sale? Choose an experimental drug to treat a disease? Get the puppy or the adult dog? We all have to make decisions within a certain time frame, and knowing those time limits can help determine the urgency.
- **Finally, what guides you in making the decision?** Is your decision consistent with your values? Does it help get you toward your goals or something that you need? Is it helpful for many people, rather than a selfish venture for yourself? Decisions are based in large part on your values, goals, needs, and relationships with other people.

Questions to Ask Yourself (continued)

1. Some decisions are relatively ________________ and don't make a big difference in your life. Others, however, are very important.
2. You should also think about how your ______________________ will affect other people.
3. Some decisions can be _______________; that is, you can change your mind if you want to.
4. If a decision is very ___________________, you might have to make a decision right away. However, sometimes you can take your ____________ making up your mind.
5. Finally, you should decide what ___________ you in making your decision—your values? Your goals? Your needs? Or your _______________ with other people?

Name____ Date______________

Worksheet 67

A Decision-Making Chart

Think of a decision you have coming up. How could this chart help you?

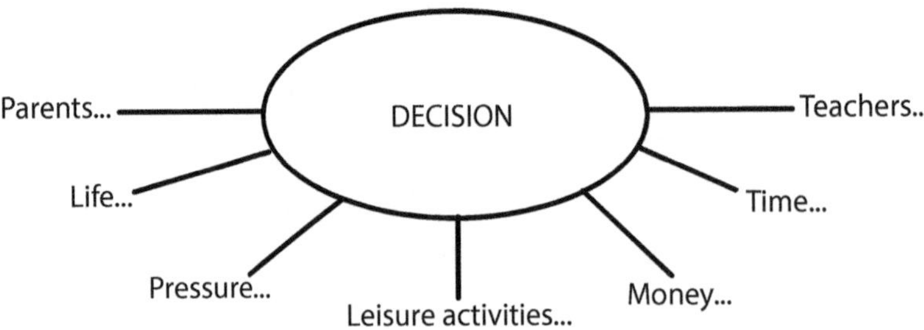
DECISION
Parents...
Life...
Pressure...
Leisure activities...
Money...
Time...
Teachers...

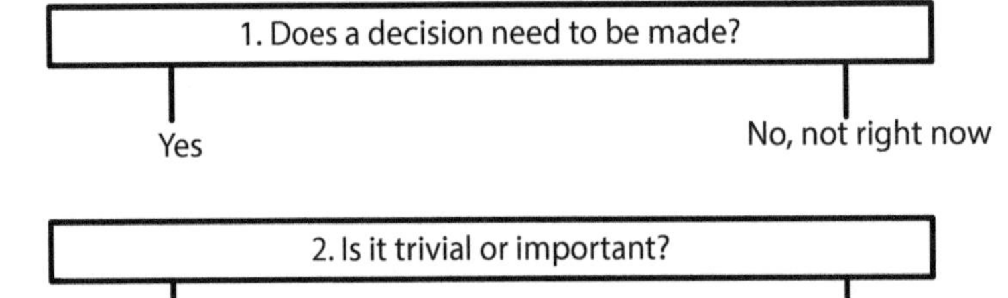
1. Does a decision need to be made?
Yes
No, not right now
2. Is it trivial or important?

Trivial

Is it reversible? Is there little risk?

Important

Are many people involved in this decision?

Do the consequences affect long-range plans?

Is this an urgent decision?

3. Do you need to get more information?

What will it cost in terms of:

- time
- commitment
- money
- relationships

Is it a real possibility for you? Are other people supportive?

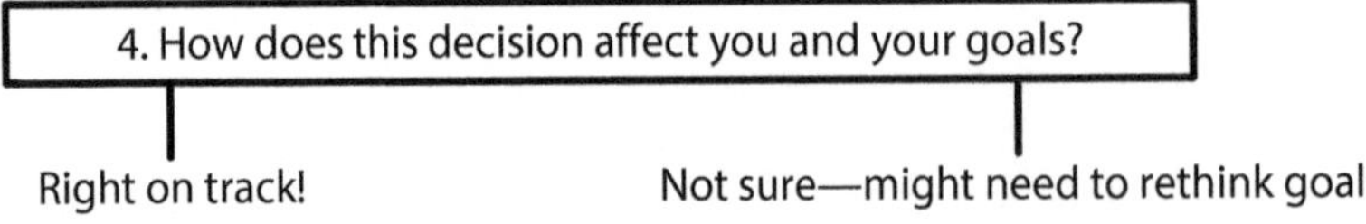
4. How does this decision affect you and your goals?
Right on track!
Not sure—might need to rethink goals!

5. What is the basis for your decision?

- right in line with what you really want
- consistent with your values
- not at the expense of other people

Name________________________________ Date____________

Worksheet 68

What Decision Needs to Be Made?

In each of these situations, someone needs to make a decision. Identify the decision in each. Use the questions on the chart from Worksheet 67 to help someone come up with a good decision.

1. Ginger, your golden retriever, is 15 years old and can't walk anymore. She seems to be in pain.

   ____

2. Grandma is 85 and can't walk anymore. She is afraid to be left alone and is in constant pain from her arthritis.

   ____

3. It's two days until graduation. Your father wants to know what you're planning to do after that.

   ____

4. The house your family has always admired has finally come up for sale!

   ____

5. Your friend Janelle doesn't want to work or go to school. She'd like to get married and have someone take care of her all the time.

   ____

6. If you agree to work overtime during the holidays, you will make extra money for every hour that you work.

   ____

What Decision Needs to Be Made? (continued)

7. You hurt your knee during tennis practice, but you have a big match coming up tomorrow.

____

8. It's late at night, you're alone, and you hear some noises outside in your front yard.

____

9. Everyone has gathered at your house, and they're all hungry.

____

10. You were out late last night and didn't have time to study for your huge history final that is during the first hour this morning.

____

Name______________________________ Date__________

Worksheet 69

When You Need More Information

What further information might these people need to make a good decision?

1. ______________________________

____

____

Wow!
This car is SOOOOOO cool! I think I can make the payments ... I love it!

2. ______________________________

____

____

There are two flights to California. One leaves in the middle of the night, but it's really cheap. And we might have to change planes three times.

3. ______________________________

____

____

Grandma sent you some birthday money. She wants you to buy a computer.

4. ______________________________

____

____

My cousin Mark wants to ask you out. He goes to another school, but he's seen your picture and likes what he sees.

When You Need More Information (continued)

5. ______________________________
____
____

You can either go out for track or play soccer. Signup is tonight after school.

6. ______________________________
____
____

If you take history in the summer, you'll probably get Mr. Peters. He's really easy and you'll have an easy A. But you probably won't learn anything.

7. ______________________________
____
____

Sure, you can drive the car, son. Just find out how much the car insurance is and let me know how you plan to pay for it!

8. ______________________________
____
____

Wow! Here's an ad for making $100 a week in cash! You can work part-time from your own home! This sounds too good to be true!

Name________________________________ Date____________

Worksheet 70

Head Versus Heart Decisions

Sometimes decisions are made impulsively—with the heart, not the head. Intuition is not always a bad thing, but don't throw common sense out the window. These decisions were made impulsively. What problems could come up with these decisions?

1. ______________________________
____
____

I think we should buy 1000 shares of this new software company. I have studied a lot about computers. I have a good feeling about this.

2. ______________________________
____
____

John is sensible, secure, and has a good job—but Ralph is exciting and carefree. He is so much fun to be with. I guess I'll marry Ralph. My parents will just die!

3. ______________________________
____
____

Oh, what a cute puppy!! He'll be so big, but our apartment is small right now. I know it says NO PETS, but we can keep him hidden. We'll teach him not to bark.

Head Versus Heart Decisions (continued)

4. ____________________
____
____

My entire paycheck is spent. But I really want that new motorcycle. I can make payments.

5. ____________________
____
____

I know I'd make more money by being a doctor like my dad, but I think I'd be happier teaching kindergarten kids. I love kids.

6. ____________________
____
____

I've got two extra tickets to the game. I know it's sold out and I could sell them ... but why don't you just take them and ask a friend to go with you? Sometime you can do me a favor!

Name____ Date____________

Worksheet 71

Not Everything Is a Crisis

How could these individuals better handle these situations? How could any of these solutions be helpful?

A = This situation can be undone or fixed.
B = Someone can help you with the situation.
C = Look for an alternative that you accept.
D = It's not as bad as you think.

1. Arthur was looking forward to eating his usual lunch of burgers, fries, and a brownie. One day the fast-food package he received had a fish sandwich instead of a burger. Arthur hates fish and was getting upset! He was ready to scream at the sales person. They offered him a coupon for a free meal at the next visit.

2. Anina realized one morning that she had forgotten to feed her neighbor's fish. She was supposed to feed them every day but one day she overslept and didn't get to it before she had to leave for school. She worried all day that the fish would die.

3. Pedro didn't understand the teacher's instructions for math homework. No one at home could help him. He threw his book on the floor and insisted that he was stupid and would probably fail the class.

4. Zora had a small scrape on her elbow from PE class and it started to bruise a little bit. She went to the nurse's office for ice and insisted that she could not go to any classes the rest of the day. In fact, she wondered if an ambulance should be called to get her to the emergency room.

5. Donnell thinks she accidentally deleted her homework after spending hours typing up a report. She texted her friend Jake, who knows a lot about computers, to ask if he could come over and help her find it. Meanwhile, she panicked and cried, thinking she had lost all that work.

Name ______________________________ Date ______________

Worksheet 72

What Is Common Sense?

GAS
GAS

Most people put their socks on before they put their shoes on. Why? Well, think about it! Some things don't make any sense until you stop to think them through. Why should you wear a coat outside when it's 10 degrees below zero? Why wouldn't you drink a cola with a lot of caffeine in it before going to bed? It seems to be obvious when you think about it. That's what common sense is all about—just using ordinary knowledge or being resourceful to solve a problem. Nothing special. Nothing out of the ordinary. Just common things that most people know and common thinking that most people can do.

Many problems can be solved by looking for clues that will give an answer—clues that are right in front of you. If your car ran out of gas in front of a 24-hour gas station . . . well, what would be an obvious thing to do? The answer may be right in front of you.

Another way to use common sense is by thinking harder about something. Let's go back to the car that ran out of gas. Take away the gas station. Would you go walking down the highway with a paper bag to put some gas in? Would you use your cell phone to call your mother in another state to come and help you out? Hey! If you have a cell phone, what's another possibility for you? Think harder!

There are many people who have common sense. They are good thinkers. They look for clues. They think harder when an idea is not right in front of them. Answers are all around you! Now find them!

1. Some things don't make any __________ until you think them through.
2. Common sense is just using ordinary __________ or being __________ when solving a problem.
3. Many problems can be solved by looking for __________ that are right in front of you.
4. Another way to use common sense to solve problems is to think about them __________.
5. Many people who are good thinkers have ____________.

Name____ Date______________

Worksheet 73

Looking for Clues

Help Charlie use common clues to answer his own questions.

1.
How do you spell November?
NOVEMBER
2.
I wonder where Dr. Smith's office is?
DIRECTORY
DR. JONES 1A
DR. PETERS 2C
DR. SMITH 30
3.
NO BOOKS TODAY TEST
Oh, no! Class has already started and I don't have my math book with me.
4.
I wonder if we're having practice outside today.
5.
Bob wants me to come to his new house. I hope I remember how to get there.
GPS
6.
Why won't this TV work?

Name______________________________ Date______________

Worksheet 74

Using Your Common Sense

What's wrong with each situation below? How could using common sense help each person come up with a solution?

1. Arnold owes $63 for book rentals, but he finds a pair of jeans on sale and wants to use the money to buy them since the sale ends tomorrow.

   ____

2. Carla is moving across the country to a new state. The day before the move, she wants to start putting together a 1,000-piece puzzle on the kitchen table.

   ____

3. The teacher asked David to do his math in pencil because she is teaching a new concept and the students will probably make mistakes. David pulls out his black magic marker.

   ____

4. Justine's cat roams all over the neighborhood and has just had its third litter of kittens. Justine knows she will have trouble finding homes for the kittens.

   ____

5. Paulina and Dustin are planning to go on an all-day bike ride out into the country. It's going to be really hot and sunny on the day they go.

   ____

6. Carmine takes piano lessons every Thursday after school. He practices on Wednesday for 5 minutes. He doesn't understand why he never seems to be getting any better!

   ____

7. Antonio is invited to a pool party on a hot day. He has fair skin and burns easily.

   ____

8. Kara has track practice after school, but she left her running shoes at home. She decides to borrow her friend's shoes, even though they are a little too small for her.

   ____

Chapter 5

Skills for Interacting with Others

Skill 13: Knowing What's Expected

INSTRUCTOR PAGES

Rationale: The ability to size up other people involves understanding what message a person is giving—whether it is spoken or implied by facial expressions, tone of voice, body language, or the sincerity of the message itself. Individuals who lack this skill are usually not aware of how others react to them or what kind of impression they are giving.

Worksheet 75: A New Kind of Reading

Students are to read the information on ways to learn about other people and then complete the sentences at the end of the worksheet.

Answer Key:

1. cover, looks 2. clues 3. clues, facial, tone, body 4. what 5. cover, person

Questions: 1. Have you ever been surprised to read a book that was nothing like it seemed to be at first? 2. Have you met any people who turned out to be very different from your first impression?

Worksheet 76: Clueing into Others' Moods

Students are to match tips for determining how a character is feeling with picture clues. The categories are facial expressions, tone of voice, and body language.

Answer Key:

Facial expressions 1. C 2. A 3. B

Tone of voice 4. E (sarcastic), D (excited) 5. G (politely shaking hands), F (enthusiastically hugging)

Body language 6. B 7. C 8. A

Questions: 1. How do these types of clues help you figure out what kind of mood someone is in? 2. Even though the words are similar, how can a tone of voice change the meaning? 3. Which tip is easiest for you to consider when you interact with someone?

Worksheet 77: Knowing What to Expect: People

Characters on this page represent various people that someone might encounter at home or on the job. Students are to read about the situation and choose which answer states what is most likely to happen.

Answer Key:

1. B 2. A 3. A 4. A

Worksheet 78: Knowing What to Expect: Situations

Students are to read over each situation, look for clues, and determine what to expect in each case.

Answers may vary.

Answer Key:

1. The locker might be empty when you come back.
2. You might have to borrow money from a friend.

3. You might run out of gas and be walking the rest of the way to work.
4. You should dress nicely and be ready to meet someone whom you might be interested in getting to know.

Worksheet 79: Knowing What to Expect: Tasks

Students are to read over the situations and decide what each person is expecting from them.

Answers may vary.

Answer Key:

1. Your mother expects you to clean up your room in a hurry.
2. Your friend expects you to help him wash his car.
3. Your teacher expects you to study over the weekend.
4. Your friend expects you to help work on the house.

Worksheet 80: Knowing What to Expect: Commonsense Clues

Sometimes you can figure out what to do without a word, simply by paying attention to what is going on. Students are to write or discuss what is expected in each situation and to underline the clue words in each item.

Answer Key:

1. The player expects a tip; coins and some dollar bills.
2. Put your napkin on your lap; everyone takes their napkin and puts it on their lap.
3. Give the hair stylist a tip; there is a jar with the word TIPS on the counter.
4. Cross the street; a lady is waving.
5. Let the dog out; your father . . . looks at you.

Name ____ Date ____________

Worksheet 75

A New Kind of Reading

You probably read a lot in school. Maybe when you go to the library to do a book report, you look for a book with an interesting cover. Maybe you look at how many pages are in the book. Perhaps you look to see who is the author, hoping that this book will be as good as their last one! Then you might open it to check out if there are lots of pictures inside or if it is filled with tiny writing. All of these are clues as to what the book might be about.

Did you know that you can also learn to "read" people? Just as you do when you assess or size up a situation by looking for and thinking about clues, you can also look for clues from other people to make good guesses as to what they are all about. What are they thinking? Are they friendly? Are they interested in you? Are you interested in getting to know them?

Some of the clues you can use to read people include looking at their facial expression (scowling? smiling?), listening to their tone of voice (loud? timid?), looking at their body language (clenched fists? arms crossed?), and listening to what they say, as well as how they say it.

You may have heard the expression "Don't judge a book by its cover." That means don't assume that just because the book doesn't have an exciting cover, it's not worth reading. It's the same with people. Don't assume that because someone seems shy or boring, they're not skydiving or tuning up their Harley-Davidson on weekends. Expand your "reading"!

What does it mean to "read" other people?

1. When you select a book to read, you might look at the ____________ to see what it's about. In the same way, you might size up the way a person ____________ to get an impression of what they are like.
2. People give ____________ as to what they are like.
3. Some of the ____________ you can use to read people are looking at their ____________ expressions, listening to the ____________ of their voice, or paying attention to their ____________ language.
4. You should notice ____________ people say as well as how they say something.
5. Don't judge a book by its ____________, and don't judge a ____________ by the way they look.

Name____ Date____________

Worksheet 76

Clueing into Others' Moods

Here are some tips to help determine how someone else might be feeling.

Facial Expressions
What emotion do you think each person is feeling? Match the letter with each feeling.

A

1. ___ surprised

B

2. ___ annoyed

C

3. ___ pleasant

Tone of Voice
What emotion do you think each person is feeling? The words are similar, but the tone is different!

4. "Oh great, we have more to do. I'm thrilled." ___
   "Oh, great! We have more to do! Fantastic." ___

D

E

Clueing into Others' Moods (continued)

5. "Nice to meet you." ___
   "I'm SO GLAD to see you!" ___

F

G

Body Language

What message is the person giving in each example? Match the message with the person.

A. "I'm kind of shy."

B. "Please don't touch me."

C. "I'm not in a good mood today."

6. ___

7. ___

8. ___

Name____ Date________________

Worksheet 77

Knowing What to Expect: People

Here are some people you might have to be around. What would you most likely expect to happen? Circle A or B.

1. Uncle Fred always likes to tease you when he comes to visit. You are really annoyed when he talks about how much you have grown, are you married yet, and all about the good old days. Here he comes to the door . . .

   Expect:

   A. *He will want to talk about his job.*

   B. *He will probably ask you if you have heard the latest political joke.*

2. Your father likes to look at your report card when it comes out and always seems to know the date that they will be available. You just got your grades and got a D in math.

   Expect:

   A. *Your father will be asking about how you can improve your grades.*

   B. *Your father will take you to a basketball game this weekend.*

3. Your best friend is usually crabby if they don't get enough sleep. You know that they went to bed early last night.

   Expect:

   A. *Your friend will be in a good mood.*

   B. *Your friend will be tired.*

4. Your boss told everyone that there will be an inspection at the restaurant in the next day or two. The last inspection did not go very well.

   Expect:

   A. *Your boss will be picky and want you to work carefully.*

   B. *Your boss will let you take off the day you wanted to be gone.*

Name____ Date______________

Worksheet 78

Knowing What to Expect: Situations

212

Read each situation and look for clues about each place. Write something that you expect might happen at each place.

Situation 1

You are going to the local gym to play basketball after school. You forgot to bring a lock for the locker, but you put your clothes, your wallet, and your iPod into the locker anyhow. It's pretty busy with a lot of people there.

What might happen?________________________________

Situation 2

Three of your friends want to go out for pizza. You realize that you don't have any money with you, but you want to go anyhow. You order food and have a good time. Then the server arrives with the check. Your friends say, "Let's just split the bill equally."

What might happen?________________________________

Situation 3

You are running late for work. You forgot to fill up your car with gas, and the little red line is below the E for empty. You know that there is always a little extra in your tank, and you don't have far to drive.

What might happen?________________________________

Situation 4

A friend of yours calls and wants you to meet his sister because he thinks you would like each other. Your friend tells you that you are going to meet at a really nice restaurant, so dress your best.

What might happen?________________________________

Name______________________________ Date__________

Worksheet 79

Knowing What to Expect: Tasks

What would each of these people expect from you if you were in the following situations described?

1. Your mother walks into your room and says, "Your Aunt Helen will be here in about ten minutes. She will be interested to see your room."

   What does your mother expect?

2. Your friend says, "What a good day to wash my car! Are you busy this afternoon?"

   What does your friend expect?

3. Your teacher says, "Class, you have a very big test coming up on Monday. I know you all want to enjoy the weekend, but don't forget about what happens when the weekend is over."

   What does your teacher expect?

4. You get a phone call from a friend who is helping build a house in the community for people who need help. He asks if you are interested in helping out because you like to build things.

   What does your friend expect?

Name____ Date______________

Worksheet 80

Knowing What to Expect: Commonsense Clues

How would commonsense clues tell you what is expected in each of the following situations? Underline the CLUE in each item below.

1. You walk past a stranger on the street who is playing a guitar and singing. There is an open guitar case on the ground with coins and some dollar bills inside it. What is expected?
2. You are at a nice restaurant with some relatives. Everyone takes their napkin and puts it on their lap. What is expected?
3. You just had your hair cut, and the girl did a really good job. As you pay for your cut, you notice a jar with the word TIPS on the counter. What is expected?
4. You are walking and come to a corner of a busy intersection. The cars are all stopped, and a lady is waving for you to go ahead and start crossing the street. What is expected?
5. Your new puppy is scratching at the door to go out. Your father puts down the newspaper he is reading and looks at you. What is expected?

Skill 14: Negotiating or Compromising

INSTRUCTOR PAGES

Rationale: Rarely in life do we get 100 percent of what we want. Especially in our dealings with others, we have to be able to give and take. This is a definite indication of maturity. Being able to negotiate with others is a way to keep relationships going well without "selling yourself out" or making the other person feel defenseless.

Worksheet 81: Negotiation as a Social Skill

Students are to read the paragraphs explaining what negotiation and compromise consist of and give an example of how someone uses these techniques. They should fill in the blanks at the bottom of the worksheet.

Answer Key:

1. Problem 2. Compromise 3. Each

Questions: 1. Do you think you are a good negotiator? Why? 2. What have you had to compromise recently? How did you work things out?

Worksheet 82: You Can't Always Have Your Own Way

Examples are given of situations in which individuals think they have more power or rights than they do. Students are to discuss why negotiation or compromise probably won't work.

Answer Key:

1. The person has a bad attitude and is making too many demands; there are many other applicants.
2. The girl is unrealistically restrictive on the boy.
3. The boy wants a car that is too expensive.
4. Time limits will not allow the boy to delay cleaning up his room.
5. Sometimes policy can't be changed.

Questions: 1. What are some reasons that you can't have your own way based on safety? 2. What are some reasons that you can't have your own way based on other factors such as money, support, interests, and so on?

Worksheet 83: Situations to Negotiate

Students are to practice acting out these situations, discuss possibilities, or write their ideas on the worksheet. Answers may vary.

Answer Key:

1. Borrow the money; pay it back with interest.
2. Agree to keep the pet out in the garage where he won't have to see it.
3. Trade the sweater, but ask for some money in addition.
4. Borrow the truck, but fill it up with gas before returning it.

5. Tell your grandmother that you will get a college degree if she helps you out financially, but you can't promise you'll be a dentist.
6. Agree that you will look presentable and won't dress exotically when you are around their friends if they don't hassle you about how you look when you are around your friends.
7. Ask if you could do the written report this time if you promise you will give an oral report the next time.
8. Talk with the coach about your situation and determine whether or not the rules can be bent for you.

Worksheet 84: Things That Aren't Negotiable

There are some situations that should not be compromised—those involving moral standards, harmful or illegal situations, and anything that an individual feels strongly about. Students are to discuss the examples and try to come up with others.

Worksheet 85: Practice Negotiating

Students can select partners or form small groups to act out negotiating in the situations on the worksheet.

Worksheet 86: Introduction to a Different Viewpoint

Students are to read several paragraphs about why individuals may have different viewpoints on a given topic, then fill in the blanks at the bottom of the page.
Answer Key:
1. Time 2. Learn or experience 3. Why

Worksheet 87: Identifying Different Points of View

Students are to discuss possible reasons why individuals in the given situations may have formed different opinions.
Answers may vary.
Answer Key:

1. The first boy may live in Los Angeles; the second boy may have a father who likes to watch football.
2. The first boy appears to be studious and probably uses the textbook a lot in his schoolwork; the girl may enjoy reading only for pleasure.
3. The first person may have worked very hard in the history class and gotten good grades; the second person may have put little effort into the class.
4. The girl may have heard that comment about blue-eyed cats; the woman obviously has an exception to that comment.
5. The girl may have a distaste for mushrooms because of the way they look; the boy has a taste for them.

Questions: 1. When have you been in a situation in which you were with someone with a very different point of view than yours? 2. Was it uncomfortable to be around someone who thought differently or was it interesting?

Worksheet 88: Changing Your Situation, Changing Your Opinion

Students are to discuss how each character has changed their opinion after time or circumstances have affected the character.
Answer Key:

1. The girl is now in a relationship.
2. The boy visited a needy country.
3. The girl got a friendly pet cat.
4. The jeans were too expensive for the girl, but then later when she had a job she could afford them.
5. The boy had a good experience with his boss helping him get a raise.
6. The girl had an accident after drinking alcohol.

Questions: 1. Why did each person on the worksheet change their opinion in each example? 2. Have you ever dramatically changed your opinion about something? Discuss.

Worksheet 89: What Are Your Opinions?

Without taking too long to think, students are to finish each sentence on the worksheet. Then they should take time to think through *why* they chose their responses. Have students discuss their reasons and whether or not they are likely to change them.

Questions: 1. Do you think your opinions are similar to others in your class/family/neighborhood? 2. What factors do you think have formed your opinions on these matters?

Worksheet 90: Being Open to New Things

Students are to think about ways that they can be flexible by being open to new things or having an open attitude about new things. Students should write their responses for each suggestion on the worksheet and think of their own examples.
Answers will vary.

Questions: 1. When is the last time you learned something new or tried something new? Discuss. 2. How can you (or others) become more informed about current events? 3. What is one way you could learn a new skill in the next week?

Name____ Date______________

Worksheet 81

Negotiation as a Social Skill

Negotiation is a real art! It involves working things out with another person (or group) so that you each get something you want, although neither side may get everything they want. Compromising is similar; this is a way that each side gives in a little bit so that both sides can have something they want. A good negotiator may not even have to compromise, but usually both sides end up giving in a little.

Little kids have this skill down pat! Watch one in action sometime. Little Susie wants to go to the zoo; Mom says she's too busy to take her. Little Susie tries her first tactic—insisting. "But I WANT to go to the zoo!" Mom holds firm: "No, I'm too busy."

Now it gets interesting. Little Susie insists even harder; the stakes are up now! "But I HAVE to go to the zoo! You HAVE to take me to the zoo!" Mom's patience is wearing thin. Her position doesn't budge. "NO, Susie. I already told you, today is not a good day to go to the zoo."

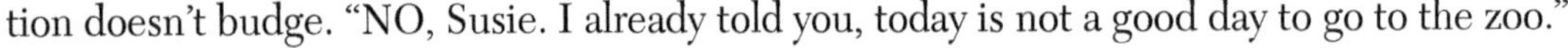

What will Susie do? Her little mind thinks, "Well, I could push even harder—try the old temper tantrum, complete with feet kicking on the floor and face turning blue . . . but that didn't work well last time. I got the famous Time Out." Susie continues to think. An idea pops into her head!

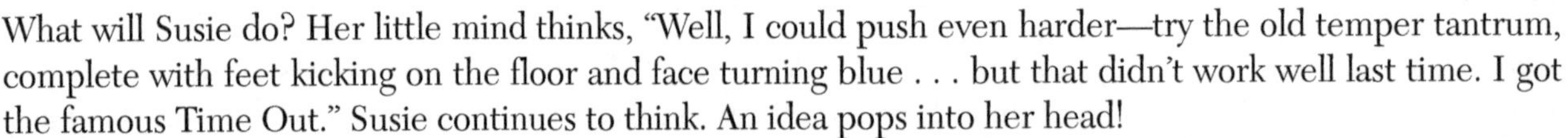

"Mom," she starts out sweetly, "I love you, Mommy." She completes the performance with a hug around Mommy's waist. "You're the prettiest mommy in the whole kindergarten."

Now it's Mommy's turn. Mommy sees through this whole act. She has to decide: (1) "Well, you're such a sweet little girl, I'll forget the housework and take you to the zoo," or perhaps (2) "Nice try, Susie, but you're still not going to the zoo today," or even (3) "I love you, too. Today's not a good day to go to the zoo, but why don't we plan to go on Saturday? We can spend the whole day, and Daddy will be able to go with us. Maybe you can even bring a friend. So why don't you find something else to do today, and we'll save the zoo for a really special trip this weekend."

How does Susie react? "OK, Mommy," and off she goes to play with her dolls.

This little drama shows that even a small child can use the process of negotiation to get what she wants. Did she end up getting her way? Well, she didn't get to go to the zoo that day, but she probably will go on Saturday. What kind of compromise was made? Susie agrees to wait and do something else; Mom agrees to delay the trip and go on the weekend.

Win-win!!

Negotiation as a Social Skill (continued)

What are negotiation and compromise, and how do they work?

1. Negotiating is working out a ______________ or situation so that both sides are satisfied with the result.
2. People can make a ____________________ as a way to negotiate a problem.
3. In a compromise, ____________________ side gives up something to the other side, but in the end both are in agreement.

Name________________________________ Date______________

Worksheet 82

You Can't Always Have Your Own Way

Read these comments by people who are not interested in negotiating or compromising. Why do you think they probably won't get everything they want?

1. Here's my application for the job. But I want my own office, a company car, and a raise every six months.

   Sure, Pal, put it over there in the stack with the others. We'll call you; don't call us.

2. We're going steady, Jorge: that means you are not allowed to talk to, look at, or be within five feet of any other female unless it is your sister, mother, or cousin.

   You're really nice, Michelle, but I still have friends who happen to be girls!

3. Dad, I really want this car. It's the only thing I'll ever ask for again! Please!

   I agreed to get you a car, but ... do you really need one that costs as much as our house?

4. Mom, I promise I'll clean my room tomorrow if you let me go to the party tonight.

   Our company is coming tonight. In about 30 minutes. Tomorrow is too late.

5. I know it says that these tickets are not refundable and that you have to use them only on this date, but it would be better for me if I could go a month from now instead of next week.

   Sorry. Company policy. Next?

Name____ Date____________

Worksheet 83

Situations to Negotiate

Here are some situations that have room to compromise. How could you get something you want in return for giving something up or doing something for someone else? Prepare to discuss your thoughts about each situation.

1. You've got a date this weekend but are low on money. You decide to try to borrow some money from your brother.
2. You want to get an exotic pet, such as a snake or a very cool-looking reptile, but your dad isn't sure he wants something like that around.
3. Your best friend offers to trade you a pair of her new jeans for a sweater that you got for your birthday. Your sweater cost a lot more than the jeans, but you don't really like the sweater.
4. You ask your neighbor if you can borrow her pickup truck to haul some trees for landscaping your yard. Your neighbor has offered to let you borrow it before, but has never taken any gas money from you.
5. You want to go to college, but you don't have the money, so you might end up working for a year or two. Then you find out that you have a rich grandmother who always wanted a dentist in the family.
6. You want to get your nose pierced, but your parents both object to this. They also objected to your dyeing your hair purple and getting a tattoo. They are so unreasonable! What can you do?
7. The teacher requires an oral report as a requirement for biology class. You get really nervous when you have to speak in front of a group and wonder if you could do something else instead.
8. The track coach says that practice is going to be seven days a week—including Sunday. You and your family always go to church on Sunday, and you work a part-time job in the afternoon. It seems that time is going to be a problem.

Name____ Date______________

Worksheet 84

Things That Aren't Negotiable

You may find yourself in situations in which you don't want to compromise and should not compromise. Can you think of some examples for the following situations?

Don't Compromise on Your Standards

I'm not going to do a really sloppy job on your car–my name goes on my work. You're going to get my best effort.
I've decided to become a vegetarian for several reasons, so my meal choices are going to be different from now on.

Don't Compromise on Things That Are Illegal or Harmful

I suppose I could cheat on my taxes—maybe I won't get caught... But I'm not sure it's worth that chance.
Don't tell me that everyone is smoking pot. I'm an example of the exception. Everyone does NOT smoke pot.
You're asking me to testify that I saw the accident and that it was not your fault. You're my friend, but I know that's a lie.

Don't Compromise on Things That You Think Are Wrong

In my religion, we believe it is wrong to drink alcohol. Please don't ask me to join you.
So I still have to take the test today? Even though I'm emotionally fragile? Can we compromise on this?

Name______________________________ Date______________

Worksheet 85

Practice Negotiating

Here are some hypothetical (but possible) situations to consider. Read them over and decide what you could, should, and would do.

1. You are the president of the ski club. Half the group wants to spend a lot of money and go to a really nice resort during spring break. The other half wants to go to two or three local resorts on three separate weekends, which would cost a lot less money. What could you do?
2. There is a gang at your school that takes money from other kids in return for NOT beating them up. You know that there are other students who resent this, but no one seems willing to speak up or take a stand against them.
3. The end-of-the-year dance has always been open to anyone from the class who wanted to go, whether they had a date or not. Now there is a group who wants only couples to attend the dance. They also think it should be formal and that everyone should arrive in a limousine. You disagree.
4. Your father expects you to take over the family business—running a funeral home. You are much more interested in going into computers and being involved in a different business. Dad won't support your efforts to do anything other than train for the family business.
5. You and your brother have to share one car while you are both in high school. Because you both have jobs, go to school, and have a fairly active social life, this can sometimes be a problem. Friday night is an example: you want to take some friends to a movie; he wants to go out on a date with his new girlfriend.
6. Your parents agree to let you have a dog, but it can't be too big, too loud, or too much trouble. You have your heart set on a St. Bernard puppy—huge, loud, and not housebroken.
7. You're at a party, and everyone seems to be drinking. You find yourself surrounded by your "friends," who tell you that if you take one drink, they'll leave you alone.
8. You and your sister both want the same dress that happens to be on sale at your favorite store this weekend. Obviously, you can't both wear the same dress at the same time or place, but you both really want it!

SALE

Name____ Date______________

Worksheet 86

Introduction to a Different Viewpoint

Believe it or not, you may not always be right! Sometimes with a little more time, experience, and thinking things through, you might find that you want to change your mind.

Let's take a look at clothes. When you have a chance, look at some old photographs of your parents. If you can control your laughter, enjoy looking at the way they wore their hair and the types of clothes they wore. Back then, they would probably tell you they were extremely stylish! But now, people would only dress that way for fun or if they wanted to have a good laugh. Time often changes the way you look at things. Yet there are still people who will insist that THAT way was the ONLY way to dress—and still is!

What about learning? Did you ever think that playing football was dumb or that science class is dull or that all cats are worthless? But what happened when you made the football team? It probably became a lot more interesting. And what about that science teacher who let your class loose in the back field to shoot off homemade rockets? Perhaps your opinion changed. And cats? Well, some people will never change their opinion about cats. But I know of someone who insisted he hated all animals, but was recently sighted patting a kitten who had curled up on his shoulder and was purring loudly. It was through experience with these different ideas that people changed their minds.

Many of us base our points of view on things that don't make sense. We believe something because someone told us to. Or because we had one bad experience. Or perhaps because we didn't take the time to educate ourselves about the subject. Take the time to think about WHY you believe what you do. You may find out that you're willing to change your mind with a little more thought.

What are some reasons why people have trouble understanding another's point of view?

1. Some people have formed an opinion a long ______________ ago, and don't want to change.

2. After people _____________ new things, they might agree that their original thinking was wrong—they just didn't realize it.

3. Another reason people stick to a point of view is that they don't even know ________ they believe what they do! It's easier just to say, "This is my opinion" than to give reasons why—even if it doesn't make sense!

Name______________________________ Date__________

Worksheet 87

Identifying Different Points of View

Each of the people in the following situations have a different point of view about the same topic. Why do you think these people feel the way they do?

1.

The Lakers are the greatest! Basketball is the best sport!

If you want to see a good sports team, it's the Green Bay Packers, all the way. There's no better sport than football. It's America's game.

2.

I can sit and browse through this textbook for hours. It's so interesting.

I can't wait to read the latest mystery novel by I.M. Scaree. I love to figure them out.

3.

Mrs. Cliff is such a fun teacher. She makes us work hard, but we have learned SO much about history this year!

All Mrs. Cliff does is think of how many types of assignments she can give us. History is boring and pointless.

4.

Any cat that has blue eyes is deaf. I've had two like that. It's really weird.

This is Fluffy. Her eyes are as blue as the sky and she always comes when I rattle her bowl.

5.

I hate mushrooms. They are so ugly and disgusting.

I love mushrooms. Load them up on my pizza!

Name____ Date______________

Worksheet 88

Changing Your Situation, Changing Your Opinion

Sometimes people change their opinions about things (people, issues, purchases, and so on) because their life situation has changed. What has changed in each of the following examples to cause the person to view things differently?

1.

I can't stand babies. They just cry all the time.

I love you! Let's start a family!

2.

I feel so sorry for the poor people in that country, but what can one person do?

Wow, visiting that country really opened my eyes to see what is needed. There are so many ways to help.

3.

Cats are so independent. They are not good pets.

I love my Petunia! She's the best!

Changing Your Situation, Changing Your Opinion (continued)

4.
I would never spend that much on jeans.
My promotion really helped! I'm shopping at the good stores now!
5.
My boss is a jerk.
Boss really went to bat for me with the management and got me a raise. Good guy!
6.
Alcohol is fun!
My car is a wreck. I didn't think I'd be out of control.

Name____ Date______________

Worksheet 89

What Are Your Opinions?

Without taking too long to think, complete each of the following sentences. When you have finished, take time to think through WHY you completed each sentence the way you did. What reasons did you come up with? Which opinions do you think you might change?

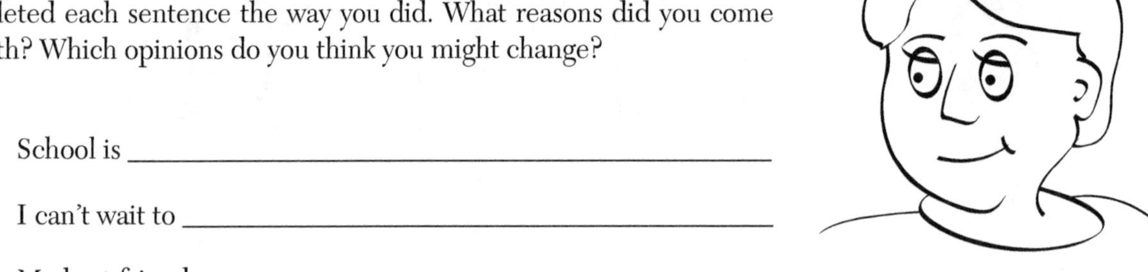

1. School is ______________________________
2. I can't wait to ______________________________
3. My best friend ______________________________
4. The best show on TV right now is ______________________________
5. I dislike eating ______________________________
6. I would give money to______________________________
7. People from other countries are ______________________________
8. Athletes are ______________________________
9. It is important to ______________________________
10. Technology makes me ______________________________
11. My favorite time of day is ______________________________
12. Being popular is ______________________________
13. People who are mean to other people should ______________________________
14. I really admire someone who ______________________________
15. Someone I'd like to get to know better is ______________________________

Name____ Date______________

Worksheet 90

Being Open to New Things

What are some ways you can

. . . LEARN something new?

I can't wait to spend the summer in Spain. I guess I should learn a few basic phrases.

____

____

____

____

____

. . . TRY something new?

White-water rafting? Me? Well ... if it's safe ... why not! I'll go!

____

____

____

____

____

. . . become more INFORMED?

Oh, come on, let's watch cartoons!

____

____

____

____

____

Being Open to New Things (continued)

. . . EXPAND your skills?

I know you like to cook. Would you be interested in joining me in a French cooking class at the Y?

. . . LISTEN to a different opinion?

Please don't make up your mind about who to vote for until you've heard what my candidate has to say!

Skill 15: Making Others Feel Comfortable

INSTRUCTOR PAGES

Rationale: You may encounter situations in which people are misunderstood, under pressure, caught in embarrassing situations, or simply in trouble. Going out of your way to try to make the individual feel comfortable (without being overbearing or nosey) is one way to be a good neighbor.

Worksheet 91: Embarrassing Moments for Others

Students are to match a technique with each situation listed.

Answer Key:

1. Use humor, give help, be sympathetic. 2. Use humor. 3. Give help. 4. Be sympathetic. 5. Use humor. 6. Stick up for him.

Questions: 1. Can you share an embarrassing moment that you or someone you know experienced? 2. What was the best way to handle that experience?

Worksheet 92: Helping Others Through Stressful or Uncomfortable Situations

Students are to share ideas for ways they could assist others.

Answers will vary.

Answer Key:

1. Help the server if she requests some assistance. 2. See if you can lend some money or talk to the coach. 3. Invite Jeanine to something else. 4. Talk to the teacher privately. 5. Tell Jon you're glad he's on your team.

Worksheet 93: Things to Beware Of!

Students are to state the problem in each situation where a character is not being helpful.

Answer Key:

1. It's potentially embarrassing for the boy—he doesn't want to talk about being in the office. 2. It's nice to just help someone out, but don't advertise it. 3. The boy just wants to figure it out by himself. 4. It is possible the girl does not want everyone to know of her situation. 5. This is not the other boy's business. 6. The girl may not be rich or want to be labeled wealthy.

Questions: 1. What is an alternative behavior for each of the situations? 2. Why might it be offensive to be too talkative, too helpful, or too involved?

Worksheet 94: Being Happy/Sad/Sharing Emotions with Others

Students are to identify which character is helping another by sharing the emotions expressed.

Answer Key:

1. B 2. A 3. B 4. A 5. B

Questions: 1. Why is it hard sometimes to be happy for other people's success? 2. Why do you think it can feel awkward to be around someone who feels sad, depressed, embarrassed, or moody?

Worksheet 95: Avoiding Hot Topics

Students are to match an example of a hot topic (one that might be controversial) with the conversations.
Answer Key:

1. C 2. A 3. C 4. B or possibly C 5. C 6. B

Questions: 1. How could each of the examples involve controversy or be upsetting? 2. Is there ever a clear RIGHT or WRONG in the topics? 3. If you are not sure of the beliefs of the people in your group, why might it be better to withhold your opinion until you know how your comment will be received?

Worksheet 96: When NOT to Be Social

Students are to state why each setting is not the right one in which to strike up a conversation.
Answer Key:

1. The lady is interested in reading her book. 2. The boy does not want to talk right now. 3. Jamie is busy doing her job and it's not a good time for Tonio to hold up the line. 4. Dalayna should be aware that her father needs some quiet time.

Questions: 1. What clues did the individuals in the examples give to show that this was not a good time to be social? 2. How could you redo each example to turn it into an appropriate social interaction?

Name________________________________ Date____________

Worksheet 91

Embarrassing Moments for Others

How could you use these techniques to help others feel comfortable during an embarrassing moment? Draw a picture or explain your ideas.

Use humor	**Stick up for them**
Give help	**Be sympathetic**

1. Abdul was walking down the steps at school when he tripped, dropped his books, and fell flat on his back in front of everyone!
2. A strange boy comes up to you, puts his arm around you, and says, "Hi, Sweetie. What's up? What??? Oh, you're not Jenny! I thought you were Jenny!!"
3. A girl in your class has a huge rip in the back of her pants that she doesn't notice . . . yet.
4. Your math teacher is reading the class's grades out loud. Donald, a boy you don't know very well, got an F. It is the lowest grade in the class. You notice Donald shrinking down in his seat.
5. Your friend is supposed to introduce you to a good-looking friend, but suddenly forgets your name.
6. The basketball coach says to your friend, "Aren't you the kid who threw the ball in the wrong basket at the game last night?"

Name______________________________ Date______________

Worksheet 92

Helping Others Through Stressful or Uncomfortable Situations

How could you smooth out these situations in which someone is stressed out or feels uncomfortable?

1.

2.

3.

4.

5.

This order is all wrong. The drinks are mixed up, the dinners aren't cooked—this is not right at all!
My first day on the job!
The uniforms cost $25. The money is due on Friday.
4
My parents can't afford that ...
I'm inviting all of the girls in the class to my party—except Jeanine.
Doesn't she know Jeanine is right here?
Today we're going to talk about suicide.
I wonder if he knows that Alan's brother attempted suicide last year?
OK, two teams!! Who wants to be captains? Start picking who you want on your team!!
No one will pick Jon. They never do!
I hate this!

Name____ Date________________

Worksheet 93

Things to Beware Of!

You have to be careful not to try too hard when trying to make someone comfortable—your help may not be wanted or needed. What's the problem in the following situations?

1.

What are you in here for? They said I cheated, but I didn't! I'm always getting picked on. It's so unfair. Last year, I ...
Be quiet!

2.

I'll be Joan's partner because I know that no one else will want to work with her. But I will. I'm just that kind of person!!
I don't want to be her partner!

3.

Do you want me to help you with that? I know the answer!!!
No, I can figure it out.

4.

Don't feel bad about being pregnant! Why, you can hardly even tell.
Now everyone will know!

5.

I notice you're taking the same medicine that my brother takes. I know it really helped him with his depression. He was practically going to jump out of a window one time!
Mind your own business!!

6.

Those are neat shoes. You must really be rich to afford shoes like that. They're really nice. Where did you get them? How much were they?
Nosey!!

Name____ Date______________

Worksheet 94

Being Happy/Sad/Sharing Emotions with Others

You can help others feel comfortable by responding to their feelings appropriately. Which character in each situation is helping by sharing their own emotions?

1.

My dog just died.

A.

Well, he was old.
It's better now.

B.

I'm so sorry to
hear that. I know you
loved him.

2.

I just won an
award for my science
project!

A.

That's great! I'm
happy for you!

B.

My brother won
an award, too.

Being Happy/Sad/Sharing Emotions with Others (continued)

3.
I'm feeling kind of sad today.
A.
Cheer up! It's a nice day!
B.
What's on your mind?
4.
I'm really excited to see what my aunt sent me for my birthday! It's always fun!
A.
Please let me know! It sounds mysterious!
B.
Are you ready to go?
5.
My coach really embarrassed me during practice today.
A.
You'll get over it.
B.
I know you try really hard. He can be tough.

Name________________________________ Date______________

Worksheet 95

Avoiding Hot Topics

When conversing with others, especially with those whom you may not know well, it is important to be aware of subjects that are controversial. If you suspect that someone will be upset or argumentative about a certain topic, think before you bring it up. Match the example with the topic type.

Topics:
A = religion
B = politics
C = personal situations

1. Anyone who thinks Slopp-o Pizza is any good is nuts. Why do you keep ordering from that place?
2. Why do you attend that church? You have so many rules! My church is a lot better than yours. You should switch.

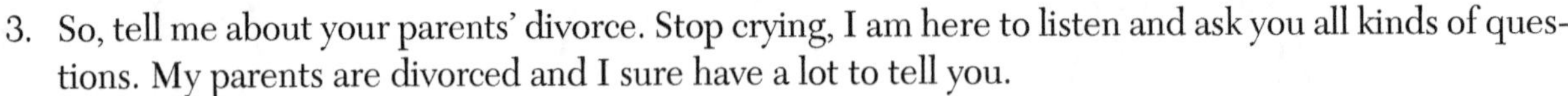

3. So, tell me about your parents' divorce. Stop crying, I am here to listen and ask you all kinds of questions. My parents are divorced and I sure have a lot to tell you.
4. The mayor of our town is a jerk. She doesn't know anything about running a city. Everything she proposes costs too much. I know she's your aunt, but still . . .
5. My mom is always nagging me about how I decorate my room. She thinks everything is a drug reference. It's my room; she should leave it alone.
6. Let's talk about that last election. I want to know if you were smart or stupid.

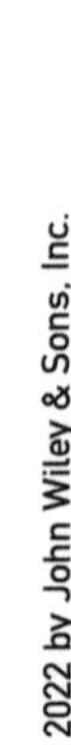

Name____ Date______________

Worksheet 96

When NOT to Be Social

Sometimes people do not want to be talked to, approached, or bothered. What is wrong with trying to strike up a conversation in these settings?

1. The public bus is very crowded and Pete has to share a seat with a woman whom he doesn't know. She is reading a book. Pete wants to show he is friendly, so he asks her where she is going. He asks her about the book. He starts to tell her about books that he has read. The woman starts to sigh and gives very short answers to his questions.

2. Raoul is walking past the detention supervisor's office when he notices a boy angrily sitting on a bench, waiting to be called into the room. Raoul knows what it's like to get into trouble occasionally, so he thought he would tell this boy about his own experiences with detention—to help him with this experience. The boy crossed his arms and put his head down.

3. It's the lunch rush at work, and Jamie is trying to stay focused on taking people's orders as they approach the counter. There are three special orders in a row and people in line are getting a little impatient. Tonio works the counter, too, but he also would like to know about Jamie's weekend. He signals his customer to wait just a second while he turns to Jamie and asks her if she went out or stayed home.

4. Dalayna's dad arrived home from work a little late one night. She finished setting the table and was getting ready to scoop spaghetti on to everyone's plates. She noticed that her dad seemed distracted and very quiet. She started to tell him about the honor society banquet coming up. Before she could finish, he said, "Not now, Dalayna. I've had a really bad day." She thought that hearing about the banquet would cheer him up.

Skill 16: Recognizing Interactions That May Not Be for You

INSTRUCTOR PAGES

Rationale: Some social interactions may not be in the individual's best interest. Peer pressure can be a very negative influence when the setting is risky or dangerous. It is also not helpful to be in a situation where you are surrounded by negative, unhappy people; people who do not respect your values or opinions; or people who do not have your best interests at heart. Students need to be aware of who is influencing them.

Worksheet 97: Everybody's Doing It

Even if a peer group gives approval to an activity, it does not necessarily mean that the activity is okay for an individual in a different situation. Students are to decide how each example might be positive for one person and negative for someone else.

Answers may vary.

Answer Key:

1. Neutral behavior 2. Think about, it's permanent 3. Might have some risk 4. Neutral behavior 5. The money might be an issue. 6. Mr. Jones may not appreciate the prank. 7. Money might be an issue. 8. Risky 9. Risky—could get in trouble for breaking curfew 10. Could be a positive activity 11. May not be important to you 12. This is vandalism!

Questions: 1. Which activities might be perceived as fun by someone but risky or mean by others? 2. Which of the examples would be easy for you to decline?

Worksheet 98: Positive and Negative Peer Pressure

Students are to read each of the comments and decide if the peers are pressuring someone to do something positive or negative. Students should write a P (positive) or N (negative) to indicate the type of peer pressure.

Answer Key:

1. P 2. P 3. N 4. P 5. N 6. P 7. N 8. P 9. N 10. P 11. N 12. N 13. P 14. N 15. P 16. N

Worksheet 99: When There's a Conflict

Students are to read about characters who are not comfortable with the conflicts they are involved in and advise them of a solution.

Answer Key:

1. Take Japanese; it's part of her long-term goal. 2. See if all of the characters could agree to do something fun together. 3. The boy could say no to the cigarette and give any number of reasons why he doesn't want to smoke. 4. This sounds like a mean prank and the boy once was in the same situation. He could choose not to participate and try to persuade the other boy to stop. 5. The girl could insist that the driver slow down or let her out—could be potentially harmful to both of them. 6. The boy could walk away from the situation by saying something like "I don't think my coach would approve. Sorry. Not sorry."

Questions: 1. Did the characters put themselves in a conflicting situation or did they find themselves in a conflict? 2. Which questions were helpful in determining what decision to make in each example?

Worksheet 100: Resisting Negative Pressure

This worksheet contains a list of ways to help deal with negative peer pressure. Students are to think of ways they could apply them to their own situations.

Answer Key:

Answers will vary.

Worksheet 101: Asking for Too Much Information

There is some information that an individual should be careful of sharing with a stranger—for example, Social Security number, bank account number, email address, and even internet sites in some cases. On the worksheet, students are to decide what information should be carefully considered before they give it to a stranger. They should be prepared to discuss a possible appropriate response to the stranger.

Answer Key:

1. A person's bank account number and balance are private information. Tell the person that you cannot give out that information over the phone.
2. Giving your address lets the person know where you live. Politely say that you can't give out that information.
3. Do not let a stranger come into your house. Get an adult or offer to make a call for him.
4. What your parents do and how much money they make is personal information. Thank the woman for the compliment on your coat and end the conversation.
5. You don't have to sign your name to anything, especially something you don't know anything about. Offer to take the information and, if you feel you want to sign the petition, sign it later.

Worksheet 102: Rude Behavior of Others

Students are to read the examples and decide which behaviors on the list show rudeness and to discuss how they could respond in each situation.

Answers may vary.

Answer Key:

1. No. She is just asking if you can help.
2. Yes. The other person is looking out only for himself; resist the impulse to honk.
3. No. Sometimes prices are not marked; it's not her fault.
4. Yes. Especially if the girl is a bad singer; try to ignore her.
5. No. Dogs will be dogs, and the owner apologized.
6. Yes. This is annoying behavior; turn around and look at him, as maybe he isn't aware of what he is doing.

7. No. She is being polite.
8. Yes. This doesn't look like a promising friendship; find another friend.
9. Yes. This is not the time or place to argue; after the lady leaves, be sympathetic to the cashier.
10. Yes. This is very inconsiderate; complain to your brother.
11. Yes. This is not her business; ignore her.
12. No. It's nice of him to offer to move down.

Questions: 1. Can you give an example of a situation in which someone was very rude to you or someone you were with? 2. How did it make you feel to observe the rudeness? 3. Did anyone step into the situation to try to change things? 4. Have you ever been the person who acted rude toward someone else? Discuss.

Name______________________________ Date____________

Worksheet 97

Everybody's Doing It

Sometimes "everybody" is really just one or two people who have influence over you. Just because "everybody" is doing something it does not mean it's right for you. Which of the following examples show situations that you might want to think about before joining in, which are neutral, and which are risky? Why?

1. ____________ ____________

We are all wearing orange to school for spirit week.

2. ____________ ____________

Let's get some piercings—ears for sure, maybe nose and lip. What do you think?

3. ____________ ____________

Who's up for skydiving? There's a special at the airport!

4. ____________ ____________

Let's put these bumper stickers on our cars. Then people will know where we go to school and what sports teams we like.

5. ____________ ____________

That dress you liked is on sale for only $500. You NEED it for that banquet. Amy and I are going shopping there for dresses, too. We will all look great!

6. ____________ ____________

Let's toilet paper Mr. Jones's house tonight! He'll think it's funny!

7. ____________ ____________

You would run a lot better if you got expensive running shoes. If you want to be a part of our team, you should get some.

8. ____________ ____________

Smoking is okay as long as you don't inhale. We've been smoking for years and we're all fine.

9. ____________ ____________

We can stay out past the curfew if we don't get caught.

10. ____________ ____________

Exercising is hard work, but we have committed to going to the gym or at least exercising outside three times a week. Join us.

11. ____________ ____________

People will laugh at you if you don't show up to prom in a stretch limo. Or at least a convertible!

12. ____________ ____________

Get your baseball bat. We're going to knock down some mailboxes while driving tonight.

Name____ Date______________

Worksheet 98

Positive and Negative Peer Pressure

Read each of the following comments. Decide which show pressure from peers to do something positive and place a P on the appropriate lines. Place an N next to the comments that show pressure from peers to do something negative.

_____ 1. "Let's join 4-H. It'll be really fun."

_____ 2. "We're all going to go to the spring dance. I know we have to invite girls, but if we all do it, it'll be OK."

_____ 3. "Everyone smokes. Here—I've got a whole pack for you."

_____ 4. "If you got your hair cut like Hannah's, your face would really show. I know where you can get it cut."

Do you think I ruined my hair?
Hey, you look fine—don't worry about it!
You may start a new fashion trend!

_____ 5. "If you want to be accepted, you'd better swear once in a while, or people will think you're a nerd."

_____ 6. "Volunteering at the hospital is a really neat experience. We can sign up after school to work there all summer."

_____ 7. "Don't talk to Debbie. We're all mad at her because she acts like she's better than we are."

_____ 8. "They're having a sale on sweatpants at the sporting goods store. We're going to wear them with our favorite baseball team shirts on Friday."

We're on the track team—and we're awesome!

_____ 9. "If a cop tries to pull me over and give me a ticket, I'll tell him a thing or two. Don't let them boss you around."

Positive and Negative Peer Pressure (continued)

_____ 10. "Our group is meeting tonight to cook a Russian meal for an extra-credit project for social studies. Join us."

_____ 11. "If anyone thinks they can beat me up, they are welcome to try it right now!"

_____ 12. "Don't buy those cheap jeans—they look awful. If you don't have expensive jeans, you'll get talked about."

_____ 13. "I don't think you should go out with Brent. He's got a really bad reputation, and I know he's been in trouble with the police. I would worry about you."

_____ 14. "I know your parents don't want you to get a tattoo, but I know where you can get one really cheap. They'll never find out."

_____ 15. "We're collecting money to send to an orphanage in Haiti. We're trying to get 100% participation for our class. Can you donate?"

_____ 16. "You can finish your homework later—we're all going to the movies tonight. Come on."

Name____ Date______________

Worksheet 99

When There's a Conflict

The following characters are not comfortable with the conflicts they are involved in. How could these questions help them make a decision:

- Does this involve a **question** or **right versus wrong**?
- Could this be harmful to me or a friend?
- Will this affect my goals for myself?

1.
Oh, take French for a foreign language. We're all taking French. Then we can talk to each other!
But I wanted to take Japanese. I hope to go to Japan as an exchange student.
2.
My cousin Ruby is staying in town this weekend, and my parents are making me take her with me all over. Could you please take her off my hands? For at least one evening?
Do we have anything at all in common? I was going to ask out Julie.
3.
Here—take a cigarette. You'll look funny if you aren't smoking. You want to be cool, don't you?
Do I?

When There's a Conflict (continued)

4.
We are playing a prank on the new kid. It'll be really funny to watch him give the wrong answers in class.
I was once the new kid at this school.
5.
I'm so terrified I can't talk.
I wonder how fast I can take this curve! Hang on! Wheeeeeeee!!
6.
If you tell on us, we'll come after you! Think about it!!
I don't want any part of this—but no one would believe me!

Name____ Date____________

Worksheet 100

Resisting Negative Pressure

Here are some ways you can resist negative peer pressure. How could you use these in situations that have happened to you?

I'd like to try surfing but I can't swim. I'll have to say no for now.

1. Find a source of strength (counselor, best friend, religion).
2. Find new friends who share your values.
3. Think of your long-range goals—don't lose sight of them.
4. Put the situation in perspective: will this matter 10 years from now?
5. Get deeply involved in something positive (volunteer work, getting straight As on your report card, sports, choir, and so on).
6. Decide to value yourself. Is it worth it to you and your reputation to give in to the pressure? Is it worth fighting?
7. Use humor to get out of the situation.
8. Don't waver in your stand: NO means NO. Practice saying it until it comes naturally!
9. Think about your reputation and what you want it to be.
10. Be a peer who puts positive pressure on others (encourage others to join you in your quests, include others in your activities, be a leader, and so on).

Name____________________ Date__________

Worksheet 101

Asking for Too Much Information

There is some information that people ordinarily do not need to give out, especially to strangers. What information is personal in each of the following examples? What would be an appropriate response to the stranger? Be prepared to discuss your responses.

1. Someone calls you on the phone and wants to know your bank account number and how much money you have in the bank.
2. A man comes up to you on the street and says he knows your family but has forgotten where you live. He asks you to tell him your address so he can find your house.
3. Someone knocks on your door after dark and says that his car broke down and that he doesn't have his cell phone with him. He asks if he could come in to use your phone to call for help.
4. A lady is admiring your jacket and asks where you got it. You tell her and then she asks if your parents are rich because it must have cost a lot. Then she wants to know how much money your parents make.
5. You are walking down the street and someone tells you that you really should sign his petition to get rid of the mayor in town. You don't really know much about the situation, but he is pushing the paper in front of you and asking why you aren't concerned about what is happening in the city. You are just one more example of someone who doesn't care about what's going on!

Name____ Date______________

Worksheet 102

Rude Behavior of Others

Students are to read the examples and decide which behaviors on the list show rudeness and to discuss how they could respond in each situation. Put a check in front of the examples of rude behavior.

_____ 1. A new neighbor asks if you would feed her fish while she is gone over the weekend.

_____ 2. You are pulling into a parking lot, and someone rushes to beat you to an open spot.

_____ 3. The lady in front of you in the grocery store needs a price check on bananas.

_____ 4. You are waiting in a doctor's office, and a girl is singing along to her music quite loudly.

_____ 5. While walking down the street, a little dog runs up to you and nips at your ankles. The owner comes up to you, apologizes, and scolds the dog.

_____ 6. You are taking an important test in a large classroom. The boy sitting behind you keeps tapping his pencil on the back of your seat.

_____ 7. In the cafeteria line, there is only one piece of chocolate cake left. A girl holds up the plate, turns behind her, and says, "Did anyone else have their heart set on chocolate cake today? If not, it's mine!"

_____ 8. A girl whom you have just met at school invites you to go skating, but when she gets a chance to go out with someone more popular, she tells you that she doesn't feel well and that she'll see you later.

_____ 9. The lady in front of you at the grocery store lets everyone know that she thinks the price of bananas is ridiculous and that the store is just trying to cheat people.

_____ 10. Your brother's friend whom you don't know borrows your car and leaves the windows open. There is a downpour! The friend asks you to please clean it up before he needs the car again tomorrow.

_____ 11. You buy a bag of potato chips. As you are munching on the chips, a lady comments, "You should be exercising, not eating junk food."

_____ 12. You go to the movies and want to sit in a seat where someone is saving a seat with a coat. You ask if that seat is available. The person says he was holding it for a friend but that they can all move down so there's room for you.

Part III

Applying Social Skills in Life Situations

Introductory Comments

Rationale: The real test of how well a person functions socially is by examining how well they adapt and control themselves in real-life settings. A person can practice social skills, but these behaviors must then be applied in a meaningful setting with a purposeful intent. This part of the book offers many examples of how a person can use social skills in several real-world settings.

Part Three is divided into six chapters with many subskills. Chapter 6, "Using Social Skills at Home," involves getting along with people in an environment that may include parents, guardians, siblings, and others who share a home.

Chapter 7, "Using Social Skills at School," provides situations that involve teachers, classes, other students, and learning remotely.

Chapter 8, "Using Social Skills at Work," has lessons on getting along with supervisors, peers, customers, or consumers, and other work-related situations.

Chapter 9, "Using Social Skills with Peers," has lessons on friendship-making, bullying, social media, and taking advantage of social opportunities.

Chapter 10, "Using Social Skills in the Community," focuses on being a part of a larger group and being a good citizen. Lessons include respecting others and their property, being aware and a part of local issues, and welcoming others to your community.

Chapter 11, "Using Social Skills in Leisure Settings," encourages students to find and engage in meaningful activities for pleasure and personal growth, such as taking advantage of joining in situations with others, adopting a hobby, and fitting in with loosely organized events.

Chapter 12 is a bonus chapter. The focus of "What Others Need to Know" is really a commentary for those who are not part of the socially struggling population, but rather for those who can assist by being good examples for students who need a good model.

Where to Go for More

SOCIAL SKILLS AT HOME

Getting Along with Parents
https://www.lifehack.org/articles/lifestyle/getting-along-with-your-parents-easy-you-follow-these-steps.html
(written for teens)

Getting Along with Family
https://kidshelpline.com.au/teens/issues/getting-along-family
(strengthening family relationships)

Getting Along with Step-Parents
https://www.wikihow.com/Get-Along-With-a-Step-Parent
(interesting step-by-step ideas for students)

Blended Families
https://www.verywellfamily.com/biggest-problems-blended-families-face-4150230
(article for adults; four biggest issues)

SOCIAL SKILLS AT SCHOOL

Asking for Help at School

https://www.teachthought.com/pedagogy/dear-students-asking-for-help-is-a-strength/
(article for educators for students of all ages)

Importance of Extracurricular Activities

https://www.crimsoneducation.org/us/blog/extracurriculars/benefits-of-extracurricular-activities/
(article for high school students)

Remote Learning Challenges

https://www.wgu.edu/heyteach/article/how-teachers-can-help-families-with-remote-learning-challenges2004.html
(article for teachers to help families with remote learning issues)

https://www.edutopia.org/article/better-breakout-room-experience-students
(for middle and high school students)

https://www.meratas.com/blog/5-challenges-students-face-with-remote-learning
(for parents or teachers)

https://www.ringcentral.com/us/en/blog/7-things-students-are-saying-about-remote-learning/
(interesting article about remote learning)

SOCIAL SKILLS AT WORK

Getting Along with Others at Work

https://smallbusiness.chron.com/5-steps-along-workplace-15602.html
(written for adults in a work environment; good tips for any worker)

First Job for Teens

https://www.verywellfamily.com/tips-for-your-teens-first-job-4065365
(tips for teens being successful at their first job)

https://www.indeed.com/career-advice/finding-a-job/best-jobs-for-teens
(helpful list of twenty best jobs for teens)

SOCIAL SKILLS WITH PEERS

Making Friends

https://www.wikihow.com/Make-Friends-Easily-if-You%27re-a-Teen
(article for teens with pictures; step-by-step tips)

https://agiletech.vn/8-making-friends-apps-to-meet-new-people-that-actually-work-2021/
(nice collection of apps)

https://www.dazeddigital.com/life-culture/article/45568/1/gen-z-making-friends-online-intimacy-myspace-instagram
(for adults; interesting insight into online friend-making)

https://www.wikihow.com/Make-Friends-Online
(easy to read, pictures, not specifically for teens)

http://nolalibrary.org/page/195/for-teens/329/websites-online-activities-for-teens
(online activities, resources, games; can share with online community)

Using Social Media

https://www.aacap.org/AACAP/Families_and_Youth/Facts_for_Families/FFF-Guide/Social-Media-and-Teens-100.aspx
(benefits and risks of social media)

https://www.mayoclinic.org/healthy-lifestyle/tween-and-teen-health/in-depth/teens-and-social-media-use/art-20474437
(tips for parents)

https://www.verywellfamily.com/benefits-of-social-media-4067431
(excellent article on how social media is beneficial to teens)

Bullying

https://www.instagram.com/theoswalsisters/
(tips and posters about bullying)

https://www.stopbullying.gov
(excellent general resource on bullying and cyberbullying)

https://parents.au.reachout.com/common-concerns/everyday-issues/bullying-and-teenagers
(resource for parents)

SOCIAL SKILLS IN THE COMMUNITY

https://www.healthyfamiliesbc.ca/home/articles/getting-teens-involved-community-activities
(benefits of getting teens involved)

https://www.winterparkha.org/10-practical-ways-teens-get-involved-community-service/
(list of good service ideas for teens)

LEISURE SKILLS

https://www.allprodad.com/fun-activities-for-teens/
(family activities)

https://www.goodhousekeeping.com/life/parenting/g32269018/fun-teen-activities/
(list of family-type activities)

https://simplicable.com/en/leisure
(comprehensive list of general leisure activities)

Chapter 6

Using Social Skills at Home

INSTRUCTOR PAGES

Introduction: This series of worksheets enables the learner to practice identifying specific social skills that can be helpful in dealing with situations that may come up in a home environment. This includes relationships with parents, other adults in the home, and siblings; home rules; and being part of a family.

Note: Answers to the worksheets will vary according to the age and developmental stage of your students. The answers provided in the answer keys are models for typical responses you should expect from your students. As with any other activity, accept answers that can be logically supported by facts.

Worksheet 103: Getting Along with Parents

The student is to identify the social skill that might be involved in getting along with parents on a day-to-day-basis.

Answer Key:

1. C 2. A 3. B

Questions: 1. What situations do you think would cause a conflict between parents and teens? 2. Do you think one side has more responsibility in resolving conflicts than another? Explain.

Worksheet 104: Getting Along with Siblings

The student is to identify which social skills could be used to respond to the situations with siblings.

Answer Key:

1. B 2. C 3. A

Questions: 1. Why is it different trying to get along with siblings than parents? 2. Do you think age or birth order makes a difference when trying to resolve issues? 3. What issues do you think most siblings fight about?

Worksheet 105: Balancing Responsibilities and Desires

The student is to read about each character who has a conflict between a responsibility and a desire. The student is to identify the conflict and then identify a helpful social skill.
Answer Key:

1. Buying a car now versus waiting to buy; using common sense
2. Doing chores versus going with friends; being flexible and being responsible
3. Getting a puppy versus no puppy; making good decisions
4. Help with sale versus babysitting; negotiating or compromising

Worksheet 106: Intrusions on Privacy

The student is to identify how some social skills could help them maintain privacy in their home.
Answers will vary.
Answer Key:
1. Being flexible, sense of humor 2. Communicating needs, using common sense 3. Compromising 4. Negotiating, making good decisions 5. Knowing what's expected 6. Rude behavior of others, standing up for yourself

Questions: 1. How do you handle issues of privacy in your situation? Where do you go to have solitude? 2. Are there rules or procedures in your house to help everyone have space?

Worksheet 107: Handling a Divorce or Family Split

The student is to identify some social skills that might be helpful in each situation regarding a divorce or family split.
Answer Key:
1. Understanding another's point of view 2. Making good decisions, understanding another's point of view 3. Understanding another's point of view 4. Controlling my emotions, viewing things realistically 5. Controlling my emotions 6. Being flexible

Worksheet 108: Living with Abusive or Dysfunctional Family Members

The worksheet lists some problems people might have in their home situation that are beyond the child's control. The student is to write examples of how social skills could be helpful in these situations.
Answers will vary.
Answer Key:

1. You might realize that there is a problem, but the other person may deny that anything is wrong.
2. You might have to put your wants or needs on hold until there is a better time to deal with them.
3. Do not allow someone else to push you beyond what is safe or good for you.
4. Even though the parent might be the one with problems, they are still an adult, and you need to be as respectful as you can be.
5. Be prepared, be aware, decide what your most healthy response should be.

Questions: 1. What help or resources are available to teens or families who are in need of support or counseling? 2. Who is a designated safe person in your life or area who could be counted on for help?

Worksheet 109: Spending Quality Time with Your Family

The student is to read each situation and determine how the families are spending quality time together and what social skills are being used.
Answer Key:

1. Encouraging each other; understanding another's point of view
2. Sharing chores; working with others
3. Playing games together; having a good sense of humor
4. Listening; being a good listener; sharing emotions with others
5. Handling time problems; negotiating or compromising

Questions: 1. What are some ways that your family gets together and enjoys each other? 2. What sacrifices have to be made in order for each member of the family to find time to get together?

Worksheet 110: Learning About Your Family

The student is to read the examples and come up with other ways that a family can learn more about its history. The student should think about using social skills such as being a good listener, being open to new points of view, changing one's opinion about situations, and other social skills that will help connect with a family.

Answers may vary.

Questions: 1. What is the best way to get to know someone? 2. How could you research the life or lifestyle of someone who is no longer living? 3. How could you initiate conversations or meetings with your own family members?

Worksheet 111: Becoming Independent

The student is to discuss how each person in the situations on the worksheet can become more independent of their family. How can the indicated social skills be helpful in their becoming independent?

Answers may vary.

Answer Key (Examples):

1. Reece needs to get a job; he could negotiate with his father to help earn some money.
2. Julia wants to do volunteer work; she could discuss her vocational interests with her family.
3. Rob needs to plan his own schedule and realize that he needs to make the decisions and know what is expected of him.
4. Carrie needs to know how to do the chores; she should take the initiative to listen and understand the task.
5. Franco wants to have more freedom; he can discuss his awareness of positive peer interactions, and try understanding his parents' point of view.

Questions: 1. Why is it important to strive toward being independent of parents? 2. What behaviors can you demonstrate now that will help you convince your parents later that you are ready for more independence?

Worksheet 112: Forgiving Others

The student is to read the situations on the page and decide which show an individual forgiving another family member.
Answer Key:

1. No; the sister is still holding a grudge about the sweater.
2. Yes; the father has forgiven the son for the accident.
3. Yes; the older sister has forgiven the brother for lying.
4. No; the first girl is still angry with her cousin for being late to her party.

Worksheet 113: Family Pride

The student is to complete the worksheet by adding the names of their immediate family members or other important people in their lives and listing at least one example of something that they are proud of.

Answers will vary.

Questions: 1. What is one example that shows you are proud of people who are close to you? 2. Have you told these individuals how you feel about them? 3. What do you think they would say when asked what they are proud of about YOU?

Name______________________________ Date__________

Worksheet 103

Getting Along with Parents

Which of the following social skills might the children in these situations use to get along with parents (or custodial adults) on a day-to-day basis?

A. Being a good listener B. Having a good sense of humor C. Understanding another's point of view

1.

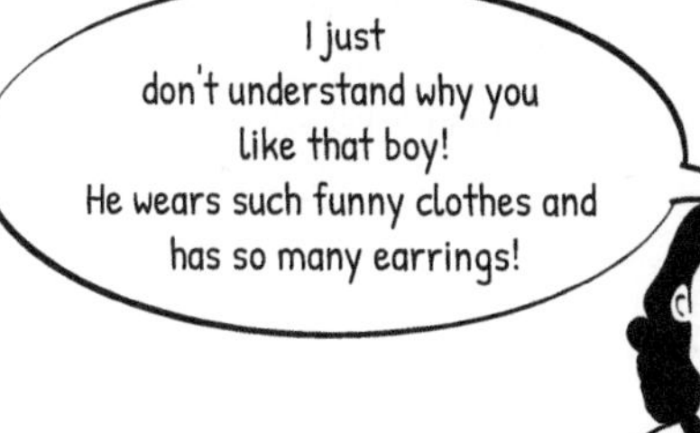
I just don't understand why you like that boy! He wears such funny clothes and has so many earrings!

2.

Let me tell you what it was like when I tried to pass Geometry 10!!

3.

I had to work overtime, I'm stressed, the house is a wreck—and you have a report card in your hand. Is this your idea of putting me over the edge?

Don't worry, Mom! No going over the edge for you! This will make your day!

Name____________________ Date__________

Worksheet 104

Getting Along with Siblings

Which social skills could you use to respond to these situations with siblings?

A. Negotiating or compromising B. Controlling your emotions C. Understanding another's point of view

1.

You broke my favorite music box! I'm going to kill you!

2.

Don't talk to me—I'm having a BAD DAY!!!

3.

We have to clean the room. Let's split it in half.
Or, I could pay you to do the whole thing.

Name ______________________________ Date ______________

Worksheet 105

Balancing Responsibilities and Desires

Each of the following characters has a conflict between something that should be done and something that they would like to do. First, identify the conflict in each situation. Then identify some social skills that would help resolve the situations. (Examples: using common sense, viewing things realistically, making good decisions)

Situation 1

Fred wants to buy a car. He doesn't have a lot of money and can't afford one right now, but he doesn't have a lot of time, either, to hold down a job to make money to buy the car.

Conflict: ______________________________

Social skill: ______________________________

Situation 2

One of Carl's chores around the house is to keep the lawn neatly mowed every week. He doesn't mind mowing, but this weekend is beautiful, and his friends are getting a group together to go to the beach for a cookout and volleyball. It's Saturday morning, and the group is leaving in about an hour.

Conflict: ______________________________

Social skill: ______________________________

Situation 3

Alison's friend's dog just had puppies—eight beautiful, little, black, wiggly babies. Alison didn't think her mother would mind if she told the friend that they could probably take two or three of them. After all, Alison intends to do all the work involved in caring for them.

Conflict: ______________________________

Social skill: ______________________________

Situation 4

Martha's family is having a garage sale this weekend. Martha promised to help organize everything and stick around to help collect all the money that will come pouring in. At the last minute, a neighbor called to ask if Martha could babysit—it's not really an emergency, but she REALLY needs to do some errands.

Conflict: ______________________________

Social skill: ______________________________

Name____ Date______________

Worksheet 106

Intrusions on Privacy

Which of these situations would be annoying to you? How could you use social skills to change or improve things? (Hint: communication, sense of humor, compromising, being flexible)

1.

Quit knocking on the bathroom door! I'll be out eventually.

2.

I'm trying to study! Keep that door closed!

3.

Brenda and I are FaceTiming. Get out of the way. Go far, far away.

Intrusions on Privacy (continued)

4.
Why do I have to babysit again? I planned to stream a good movie tonight.
5.
I'm just here to work. Why are you asking me all these personal questions?
6.
You read my JOURNAL? How could you?!

Name________________________________ Date______________

Worksheet 107

Handling a Divorce or Family Split

What social skills might be helpful in these situations?

1.

I don't want Dad to leave.
Can't you just
stay together?

____
____
____

2.

I'm moving in with Mom.
She's a lot easier to
deal with!

____
____
____

3.

I'm going to have to
go back
to work. Everything will
be different for us.

____
____
____

4.

Stepbrother? What's all
this about a stepbrother?
I LIKE being an
only child!

____
____
____

Handling a Divorce or Family Split (continued)

5.

WHAT? Mom's going
to get married?
No way!!

____

____

____

6.

Half a year with Mom,
half a year with Dad,
I hate it. I don't think
it's fair.

____

____

____

Name ______________________________ Date ______________

Worksheet 108

Living with Abusive or Dysfunctional Family Members

Some people in your home may have problems that are beyond your control. Examples of problems:

Alcoholism

Depression

Extremely bad temper

Being unable to work, disabled

Looks like Dad's really out of it. This is not a good time to ask for help with my algebra!
BEER

How could these social skills help?

1. Understanding another's point of view

____

____

2. Being flexible

____

____

3. Standing up for yourself

____

____

4. Respecting authority

____

____

5. Controlling my emotions

____

____

Name________________________________ Date______________

Worksheet 109

Spending Quality Time with Your Family

How are these families spending quality time together? Which social skills are they using?

1.

Go, Kara! Run!! You can do it!

Hang in there, sis!! Go, go, go!!

____
____
____
____
____

2.

You're so thoughtful.

____
____
____
____
____

3.

We've all had a hard week—let's have some fun.
Okay, it's Tova and I against you and Mom. Flip to see who goes first!

____
____
____
____
____

Spending Quality Time with Your Family (continued)

4.

I'm really disturbed about something one of my friends is doing. Can we talk about it over dinner?
Sure, let's do that.

____
____
____
____
____

5.

Kids, I have to work late every night this week, but let's all agree to save Saturday to go to the movies together.
Yeah!
Deal!!

____
____
____
____
____

Name________________________________ Date__________

Worksheet 110

Learning About Your Family

What are some ways (or places or situations) in which someone can learn more about their family? Add a few of your own ideas. Discuss how these social skills could be helpful.

Being a good listener

Being open to new points of view

Changing your opinion

1. Reading old journals or diaries from your grandparent's attic
2. Attending a funeral
3. Visiting relatives
4. Writing to a cousin
5. Attending a family reunion
6. Tracing your family tree
7. Going through old photo albums or watching old home movies
8. Interviewing people who knew your parent or relatives
9. Reading about the time period/historical account of when and where your ancestors lived
10. Taking your mother/father/sibling/grandparent/distant relative out for lunch to chat
11. Attending activities that your siblings are involved in
12. Playing games that involve asking questions of each other
13. ______________________________
14. ______________________________
15. ______________________________

Name______________________________ Date______________

Worksheet 111

Becoming Independent

Discuss ways that each of the following people can become more independent of their family. How can the social skills indicated be helpful?

1. Reece is tired of always having to ask his father for money to put gas in the car. He thinks that his father is tired of giving him money, too. (knowing what to expect, negotiating or compromising)

2. Julia wants to volunteer to teach reading at the library after school to see if she would like to be a reading teacher sometime. Her mother thinks that she is already too busy and that this is a waste of time because Julia won't get paid. (standing up for yourself, controlling your emotions, communicating)

3. Rob's mother writes his homework assignments and tests for him on the family calendar. She helps him remember to study for each test. (making good decisions, using common sense)

4. Carrie's older sister explained how to sort the clothes before doing the laundry. Carrie was watching TV while her sister was talking and didn't sort the clothes at all. (being a good listener, knowing expectations)

5. Franco is tired of his parents worrying about how late he is staying out and who he is with. He thinks they don't trust him, but he is with good friends who don't get into trouble. (resisting negative peer pressure, understanding different points of view)

Name____ Date______________

Worksheet 112

Forgiving Others

Are these individuals forgiving a family member for something that happened?

1.

Can I borrow your sweater?

Remember what happened the last time you borrowed my clothes? Forget it!

2.

Dad, can I take the car tonight?

Yes, I will be. Thanks for letting me have it even though I backed into the garbage can.

Sure, son, I know you will be careful.
We learn from our mistakes.

Forgiving Others (continued)

3.
I am really sorry that I lied to you, Sis.
It's over. We'll move on.
4.
You were late to my party.
It really bothers me.
I am really sorry about that.

Name______________________________ Date______________

Worksheet 113

Family Pride

There is always something that you can be proud of in your family. What is something that your family members have done or something else about them that you are proud of?

My father . . .

My mother . . .

Sisters . . .

Brothers . . .

Aunts, uncles . . .

Grandparents . . .

Other family members . .

Chapter 7

Using Social Skills at School

INSTRUCTOR PAGES

Introduction: The school environment requires a different set of social skills than those needed at home. In a home environment, the student must fit into a family unit with probably only a few adults to answer to. At school, there are many other peers who have needs and personalities, some of which are not compatible with the student's. There are also multiple teachers and other adults who have a say in what goes on. There are structured tasks that must be accomplished. There are procedures, deadlines, expectations, and the needs of others who also fit into this environment. Getting along with others at school is a very important training ground for later environments, such as work or the community.

Note: Answers to the worksheets will vary according to the age and developmental stage of your students. The answers provided in the answer keys are models for typical responses you should expect from your students. As with any other activity, accept answers that are reasonable or can be explained.

Worksheet 114: Getting Along with Teachers and Other Authority Figures

The student is to read the situations and list a social skill that would be helpful in each case. All items involve a teacher or adult authority figure.

Answers will vary.

Answer Key:

1. Being a good listener 2. Reacting appropriately to cafeteria staff 3. Using communication skills 4. Knowing expectations 5. Being flexible 6. Making good decisions 7. Controlling emotions 8. Making a good impression 9. Making good decisions 10. Standing up for yourself; using common sense

Questions: 1. What are some common problems that teens would have with teachers or authority figures at your school? 2. Are there some teachers who are particularly challenging to get along with? 3. What are some ways you could improve those relationships?

Worksheet 115: Managing a Social Life

The student is to look over the social calendar of a character and make suggestions or comments as to any changes.
Answer Key:

Monday: skip the movie, because it's a school night.
Tuesday: it's a busy day, but no time has been set aside for studying.
Wednesday: another late night.
Thursday: skipping school that day? Maybe rethink that.
Friday: busy day, but seems manageable.
Saturday: a fun day.
Sunday: hope he can catch up on everything.

Questions: 1. Why is it important to balance a social life with your school life? 2. What activities are you more willing to hang on to? 3. What helps you make decisions about how your social time will be managed?

Worksheet 116: Asking for Help

The student is to read over the situations and decide which social skill would help each character on the worksheet.
Answer Key:
1. C—giving space 2. A—good first impression 3. B—controlling emotions 4. D—knowing what's expected
Questions: 1. What help did each character on the worksheet need? 2. If you were rewriting each scene, what conversation would you change in each?

Worksheet 117: Eating Lunch Alone

Students are to write or discuss how each character on the worksheet probably feels about eating lunch alone.
Answer Key:
1. Not particularly worried about eating alone 2. Fearful, afraid of being judged 3. Has a plan to leave the lunchroom every day 4. Joins a group of other students who are welcoming to all 5. Makes an effort to invite someone to lunch so he doesn't have to sit alone
Questions: 1. Is sitting alone at lunch an issue at your school? 2. How could you assist someone who didn't want to sit alone? 3. Do you prefer sitting alone to eat sometimes rather than sitting with others?

Worksheet 118: Failing Classes

The student is to read over the information about the characters on the worksheet who are having difficulty in school and list a way that the social skill suggested might help them improve.
Answer Key:

1. Listen more carefully; take notes.
2. Share the load.
3. Stay home and get the work done first.

4. Realize that each grade is important; a lot of things might happen to interfere with getting the needed A on the test.

Questions: 1. Have you ever been in danger of failing a class? 2. What steps could you have taken to change the situation?

Worksheet 119: Discipline Problems

Which skill(s) might help the students on the worksheet get along in matters of discipline at school? The student is to write the letter of the skill next to the example of a student having a discipline issue at school.
Answer Key:

1. C (showing disrespect for the teacher by talking back)
2. D (giving in to anger by tearing up the paper)
3. A (they are still going to get in trouble whether they are on school property or not, but they may have to answer to the police instead of the principal)
4. B (making a good impression, respectable language)

Worksheet 120: Intimidation from Other Students

The student is to read over the situation on the worksheet in which one girl is trying to intimidate another. What skills did the second girl use to resolve the situation?

Answer Key: First she tried to defend herself, but the other girl was not really listening to her. The girl continued to embarrass her, but she stood up for herself. Then she decided to control her emotions and walk away. She did not respond to the rude behavior of others.

Worksheet 121: Developing a Bad Attitude Toward School

The worksheet shows characters who are making comments that reflect a bad attitude toward school. The student is to write advice or a suggestion for each character.
Answer Key:

1. A good education will help you get a better job.
2. Are you asking questions if you don't understand?
3. Don't let others ruin your opportunity—or be an excuse.
4. Ask for extra credit or try to do independent projects.
5. Plan to be awake when the instruction is available.
6. Is that your life goal? Is it realistic?
7. What if you start missing more than you can handle?
8. That shows a lack of effort. What does that say about you as a worker?

Worksheet 122: Extracurricular Activities

What extracurricular activities are available at your school? The student is to think about activities that they would like to have added. Discuss how these activities make school a more pleasant social place for students.
Answer Key (Examples):

Grandparent's Day, Career Week, tour guides for new students, banquet for school volunteers

Questions: 1. How does getting involved in extra activities help you become a better all-around student? 2. What activities interest you? 3. If you could create new activities, what would you be interested in seeing available at your school or in your community?

Worksheet 123: Giving Extra Effort Toward Excellence

How could the characters on the worksheet strive toward excellence—going beyond what is expected in these situations? The student is to offer suggestions on the lines provided.
Answer Key:

1. Add length, references, visual aids.
2. Make a poster.
3. Have an interesting cover that will catch the reader's attention.
4. Take candid photographs of students at school, have them framed, make a collage, and so on.
5. Slow down, be extra careful.
6. Do the best job at being a manager, cheer for the team, avoid complaining.
7. Use bright colors, do a rough draft first, be neat, label the states accurately and clearly.
8. Have place mats and napkins, flowers on the tables, and so on.

Worksheet 124: Work-Study Options

Some schools offer credit for work-study positions. The student is to discuss the possible jobs in their school or community at which students can work while attending school. Students discuss how this helps both the worker and the employer.

Answers will vary.

Answer Key:

1. Can observe the technical parts of the job 2. Being aware of what jobs are available at the hospital 3. Realizing how much is involved in completing a construction project 4. Testing organizational office skills 5. Deciding if you like working with children 6. Observing how a bank helps meet the needs of students and the community

Questions: 1. How does a work-study program benefit the student? 2. How does this type of program benefit an actual business? 3. What work-study opportunities are available in your community?

Worksheet 125: School Safety

What social skills would be important in each school safety situation listed? The student is to write the letter of the social skill in the box for each situation.
Answer Key:

1. D (following procedures for a fire drill) 2. A (this is not the time to argue) 3. B (this person already isn't following school procedures) 4. C (being calm in a frightening situation might also help others)

Questions: 1. What could happen in each situation if procedures were not followed? 2. Do you feel safe at your school? 3. What could be done or improved to ensure greater safety at your school?

Worksheet 126: Remote Learning

Remote learning can have its issues. Students are to select the answer that provides a reasonable solution to each problem.

Answer Key:

1. A (eliminate distractions) 2. B (students are still responsible for the information they are supposed to learn) 3. B (walking around might help him focus when he sits down again) 4. A (take the initiative to find out more information in something she is interested in) 5. A (if the class is online, they could meet in an online venue) 6. B (she should make an attempt to participate) 7. A (clear the desk of distractions) 8. B (find someone who is likely to have the information she needs)

Questions: 1. Some students have little trouble adjusting to remote or distance learning because they are already familiar with the technology used. Others have to acquire new skills to adapt. Where do you see yourself on this issue? 2. What aspects of remote learning are most difficult for you? 3. What parts of remote learning do you like or enjoy?

Name______________________________ Date__________

Worksheet 114

Getting Along with Teachers and Other Authority Figures

Which social skills would be important in the following situations involving teachers, principals, and other authority figures that would be encountered at school?

1. Planning your course schedule for next year

   ____

2. Eating lunch in the cafeteria

   ____

3. Not understanding a teacher's assignment

   ____

4. Being in a class and listening to a "boring" lecture

   ____

5. Dealing with a teacher who always seems to be in a bad mood

   ____

6. Being told to quiet down in the auditorium

   ____

7. Being told to quiet down on the bus on your way to school

   ____

8. Passing a teacher in the hallway

   ____

Getting Along with Teachers and Other Authority Figures (continued)

9. Responding to invitations to work on a committee for your class

____

10. Being called into the office to report on what you saw concerning vandalism in the school

____

Good morning, Mrs. Brown! See you in class!
With your homework done, of course!
Of course!
What a nice young man!

Name____ Date_______________

Worksheet 115

Managing a Social Life

What do you think of Jerry's social calendar for this week? Does he need to make any changes? What would you suggest?

Monday

7:30 a.m. Class committee meets to work on Spring Dance idea

Noon Eat with Debbie in cafeteria

3:00 p.m. Meet with counselor to plan bulletin board for hallway

4:00 p.m. Baseball practice

6:00 p.m. Go to the movies with Norm, Joey, and Tom

9:00 p.m. Study with Arnie

Comment/suggestion:

____

Tuesday

6:00 a.m. Jogging with Nabil

7:30 a.m. Class committee meets for breakfast

Noon Eat with Sandy in cafeteria

3:30 p.m. Work out at the YMCA with the guys

5:00 p.m. Stop by nursing home to see Grandma

6:00 p.m. Dinner with family

7:30 p.m. Return phone calls to friends

9:00 p.m. Watch TV movie with Steve

Comment/suggestion:

____

Wednesday

6:00 a.m. Jogging with Nabil

7:30 a.m. Class committee meets to work on Spring Dance decorations

Managing a Social Life (continued)

Noon Eat with Alicia in cafeteria

3:00 p.m. Math Whiz Club meets

4:00 p.m. Baseball practice

6:30 p.m. Volunteer at animal shelter

8:00 p.m. Dinner with new girl in class

Comment/suggestion:

Thursday

6:00 a.m. Skip school; leave for amusement park with the guys

9:00 p.m. Collapse!

Comment/suggestion:

Friday

6:00 a.m. Jogging with Nabil

7:30 a.m. Meet with class committee to work on decorations

Noon Eat with Yolanda in cafeteria

4:00 p.m. Baseball game

7:30 p.m. Dinner with the team

Comment/suggestion:

Saturday

6:00 a.m.–10:00 p.m. All-day field trip with baseball team to major league baseball game

Comment/suggestion:

Sunday

Sleep in, do homework, do laundry

Comment/suggestion:

Name____ Date____________

Worksheet 116

Asking for Help

How could these social skills be useful for students who are in need of help?

A. Making a first impression

B. Controlling emotions

C. Allowing personal space

D. Knowing what's expected

1.

Hello, Jerry! Would you mind handing me those carrots?
Oh, I'm sorry. I didn't realize I was in your way.

Asking for Help (continued)

2.

3.

4.

Mr. Langford, my name is Dori, and I'm working on a paper about our town's history. Can you answer some questions for me?
Absolutely! That's my hobby.
This computer isn't working right. I hate computers!!
It's broken!!! It's going to mess everything up. Why isn't it working?
Why don't you let me demonstrate this for you? Don't bang on it.
I TOLD you not to bang on it! Let me know when you're ready to be helped.
What's your problem, Sue?
Well, what don't you understand?
Do you have any idea what you're supposed to be doing?
I don't know?
Ummm, I don't know.
I need help! That's why I'm here! Why won't you help me?

Name ______________________________ Date ______________

Worksheet 117

Eating Lunch Alone

How do these students feel about eating lunch alone?

1.

I'm here to EAT LUNCH. That's it. I don't want to talk to anyone. I just want to have a little space and quiet myself down. No chatter, no questions ... I'm perfectly fine eating my lunch by myself.

2.

I feel as though I'm being judged. If I'm by myself, it means I'm unpopular and there's something wrong with me, right? I'll play on my cell phone or read a book. If someone comes up to me, that's fine, I'm happy to talk. But I need my props.

3.

I have an arrangement with the lunch teacher that I can go to the library or another space at school as soon as I have finished eating. I don't have to sit there and just watch the time go by.

Eating Lunch Alone (continued)

4.
Sometimes a group of loud kids will yell out "Sit with us!" to anyone who looks like they are desperate for someone to sit with. They are not mean kids; in fact, they have a great sense of humor and make everyone feel welcome.
5.
I try to invite someone to eat with me sometimes. There are some kids with common interests in my English class and also in my after-school chess club. If I don't want to eat alone, I will make an effort to ask one of them to talk through a project with me.

Name________________________________ Date______________

Worksheet 118

Failing Classes

These students are having difficulty in their classes at school. How could these social skills help them do better?

1. Being a good listener

I never seem to know what my assignments are or when they are due.

2. Working with others

I know we were supposed to work on the project as a group, but I was too busy, so I guess I didn't turn in my share.

3. Making good decisions

I would much rather go out with my friends than stay home on a weekend and study! Come on!

4. Knowing expectations

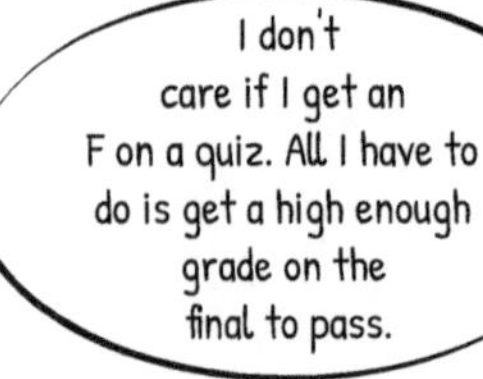
I don't care if I get an F on a quiz. All I have to do is get a high enough grade on the final to pass.

Name____ Date______________

Worksheet 119

Discipline Problems

What skill(s) might help the following students get along in matters of discipline at school?

A. Using common sense B. Making a good impression

C. Respecting authority D. Controlling my emotions

1.
Well, I have another detention after school for talking back to the teacher, but I don't care. I told him off!!!
2.
Another write-up for not having my assignment done? Again! I'm just going to tear it up. I'm not going to do it. I don't care if I get in trouble.
3.
Johnny and I are planning to fight those creeps after school. We just have to stay off of school property and we'll be okay.
4.
I can't believe I got in trouble for using swear words. Everybody swears around here. Why should I get in trouble for that?

Name ______________________________ Date ____________

Worksheet 120

Intimidation from Other Students

How did the second student handle this situation in which another student tried to intimidate her? What skills did she use?

Wow, you look great today! Who are you trying to impress?
Well, I'm giving a speech fifth period. I wanted to look nice, okay? So what?
Miss Goody-Two-Shoes. Trying to get a good grade from Mr. Schoof? Everybody knows you flirt with him.
I do not. I like him as a teacher.
Flirt.
Oh, come on. Forget it.
No, wait. There's a lot of us who don't like the way you act in class. You're always trying to be better than us.
I'm really getting mad, but I'm going to walk away!
Well, I'm sorry you feel that way. I'm just trying to do my best in a subject that I enjoy.
Smarty pants.
Good-bye.

Answer: ______________________________

____

____

____

____

____

Name ______________________________ Date ______________

Worksheet 121

Developing a Bad Attitude Toward School

Read these comments that reflect a bad attitude toward school. What advice might you give to each person?

1. School is stupid. What does it do for anyone anyhow?

   ____

   ____

2. These teachers are so dumb—they don't care if we do well or not. No one tries to explain anything so you understand it.

   ____

   ____

3. How can you learn anything when there are gangs and drugs and kids who don't know how to behave in your classes? It makes me want to quit.

   ____

   ____

4. I really try hard and I resent it when the kids who don't care in the class slow us down or get us off track. I don't like learning with other kids.

   ____

   ____

5. I don't really wake up until after lunch, so whatever happens in my morning classes is wasted on me!

   ____

   ____

6. I can't wait to quit school. I'm going to open up a video game store and make lots of money playing games all day.

   ____

   ____

7. It doesn't matter if I miss a day or two each week. I can get the assignments and make them up.

   ____

   ____

8. All I have to do is pass my classes. I don't care if I get As—I just can't get any Fs. I'll do the minimum amount of work I have to do to get by!!

   ____

   ____

Name____________________ Date__________

Worksheet 122

Extracurricular Activities

What extracurricular activities are available at your school? What are some activities that you would like to see added? How do these activities make school a more pleasant social place for students?

- Sports
- Art club
- Drama club
- School play
- Foreign language club
- Working on the yearbook
- Volunteering at the hospital
- Volunteering at a nursing home
- Pep club
- Managing a sports team
- Chess club
- Painting murals on the wall
- Peer tutoring
- Tutoring younger children

Can you list some other activities?

____

____

____

____

____

Name____ Date_______________

Worksheet 123

Giving Extra Effort Toward Excellence

How could these students strive toward excellence—going beyond what is expected—in these situations?

My masterpiece!

1. Toni got a C+ on her research report. It is five pages long, and she used only one reference. There are no pictures.

   ____

2. Ming is giving an oral report on an inventor. He is supposed to give a three- to five-minute report with at least one visual aid.

   ____

3. Arthur has written a creative story. He plans to have his sister type it up so it will be easy to read.

   ____

4. Mia is taking a photography class. She is supposed to turn in 12 photos in some sort of display.

   ____

5. Marcos helps the school janitor clean up the cafeteria after meals. He usually hurries through his job.

   ____

6. Nasim is one of the managers for the girls' basketball team. She is responsible for scorekeeping, getting water for the players, and running errands. She wishes she had made the team, because several of her friends did.

   ____

7. Will's social studies teacher asked him to design and paint a map of the United States on the wall.

   ____

8. Amy's home economics group is preparing a tea for the teachers during Appreciation Week. She is supposed to plan activities for this event.

   ____

Name____________________________ Date____________

Worksheet 124

Work-Study Options

Sometimes a student can get credit for working while going to school. Here are some possible jobs that might count for credit. How might each of these jobs help the student? What are some other possibilities in your school or community?

1. Working as a supervised car mechanic in a local garage
2. Helping the hospital volunteer coordinator a few times a week
3. Being part of a construction crew in shop class to build a house
4. Working as a secretary or office helper in a local business office
5. Helping a teacher in an elementary classroom a few times a week
6. Participating in a business program for students at a local bank
7. ____________________________
8. ____________________________

Name____ Date____________

Worksheet 125

School Safety

What social skills would be important in each of the following situations?

A. Respecting authority
B. Using common sense
C. Having a good sense of humor
D. Knowing expectations

Situation 1

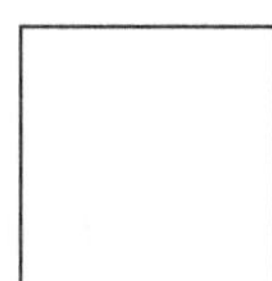

The fire alarm has gone off. You don't know if it is a drill or not, but you're supposed to line up and exit the building. You immediately get up and get in line without talking.

Situation 2

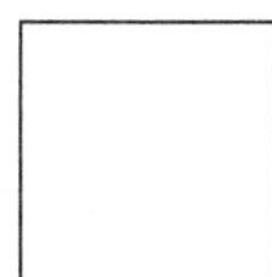

There is a lockdown announced. Everyone is supposed to be quiet and follow instructions from the teacher. You are in the gym, and you live close to the school. You want to just leave the school and go home because you know that it is a safe place. They tell you that no one is allowed to leave, so you begin to argue with the teacher.

Situation 3

You are walking down the hall on your way to the office when a person you don't know asks you where the principal's office is. You think this is odd because all visitors are supposed to stop in at the principal's office when they come to school. You stop a teacher and let her know that this person needs some help.

Situation 4

There is a tornado warning in your area. Instead of leaving at the regular time, all students have to sit in the hallway and wait for the all-clear signal. You were supposed to go to a dentist's appointment to get a cavity filled, so you aren't too sad about being delayed. You tell the teacher that you really didn't plan this tornado just so you could get out of going to the dentist.

Name________________________________ Date____________

Worksheet 126

Remote Learning

Each of these students is experiencing something that is interfering with their remote learning experience. Which answer shows a reasonable solution?

1. Yves is trying to pay attention to the teacher on the screen, but his sister is cooking in the background and the dog is barking.
   A. He should find a quiet spot away from distractions.
   B. He should stop listening to let the dog out and find out what's for dinner.

2. Francine was supposed to check in online for her class, but she overslept and missed it.
   A. She should just forget about it.
   B. She should find out what information was missed and complete any assignments.

3. Benito is very bored with watching his classes online. He feels like falling asleep.
   A. He should just take a nap.
   B. He should take some movement breaks to walk around the room.

4. Denise is very interested in her remote learning science unit about space travel. She would like to learn more about photography of Mars and space technology, but she isn't sure what to do about it.
   A. She should contact the teacher for further resources.
   B. She should hope that there will be more lessons about space sometime.

5. Alex misses talking with his friends in person. He would like to propose a class project to make up a class theme song, but he isn't sure how to get everyone together.
   A. He could suggest working in a breakout room with peers who are interested in this project.
   B. He could ask if interested people could meet together somewhere, even though he knows this is against the school rules.

6. While on Zoom, Samantha does not want to contribute to discussions. She'd prefer to just watch.
   A. She should try to look involved but not say anything.
   B. She should make a goal to participate at least two times every session.

Remote Learning (continued)

7. Tomas has all kinds of objects on the table where he sits for remote learning. He thinks if he gets bored he might take a few minutes to play Candy Crush or sketch some motorcycle cartoons.
   A. He should move everything off of the table except for needed supplies and maybe a plant.
   B. He should keep a jigsaw puzzle handy for when he gets bored.
8. Keeley isn't sure she understands what's expected for her English assignment. She watched the video but isn't sure of what she is supposed to do.
   A. She should just skip it until tomorrow.
   B. She should check with a peer to see if someone else knows.

Chapter 8

Using Social Skills at Work

INSTRUCTOR PAGES

Introduction: Finding and maintaining a job is a crucial life task that usually follows the school years. For special needs learners, many jobs may not be appropriate or possible for someone with a disability. Good social skills might be the deciding factor when an employer is considering hiring someone for a job, especially if that job involves interaction with others. In the world of work, the learner now has to get along with supervisors, peers, customers or consumers, and people who get him to and from work, answer his questions at work, or are somehow otherwise involved in his work setting. The learner also has to know how to dress, act, respond, and communicate in this environment.

Note: Answers to the worksheets will vary according to the age and developmental stage of your students. The answers provided in the answer keys are models for typical responses you should expect from your students. As with any other activity, accept answers that can be logically supported by facts.

Worksheet 127: Getting Along with Your Supervisor

The student is to read over each work situation involving a supervisor and identify at least one social skill that might be helpful on the job.
Answer Key:

1. Using good communication skills
2. Understanding another's point of view
3. Being a good listener
4. Understanding another's point of view
5. Making a good impression
6. Making good decisions

Questions: 1. Why is it important to be able to see a job from the supervisor's point of view? 2. Why should you respect authority even if you disagree with your supervisor?

Worksheet 128: Getting Along with Coworkers

The student is to determine what social skills might help each character on the worksheet get along with the people they have to work with.
Answer Key: Answers may vary.

1. Negotiating or compromising
2. Controlling emotions
3. Knowing expectations, having a private conversation
4. Knowing expectations, making good decisions
5. Being flexible, knowing expectations, respecting authority
6. Knowing expectations, using common sense

Questions: 1. Different types of jobs might require different expectations for coworkers. Can you give some examples? 2. How could a coworker make a job easier? Worse?

Worksheet 129: Is This the Right Job for You?

Students are to read over the examples of characters who are not a good match for their job. Discuss what skills are important for each job.
Answer Key:
1. Not a good match—does not like interacting with children 2. Not a good match—afraid of horses, maybe should find a different job at the ranch (housekeeping? clerk?) 3. Not a good match—disorganized 4. Not a good match—the server does not know the menu options 5. Not a good match—is not interested in the job or staying at the job

Questions: 1. What type of job might be a better fit for each of the characters? 2. What could each character do in order to become better at the job? 3. Is it OK to stay at a job you don't particularly like? For what reasons?

Worksheet 130: Understanding the Skills Required for the Job

The student is to identify what skills (not necessarily social skills, but job skills) might be required in order to perform the jobs well.
Answers will vary.
Answer Key:

1. Being responsible, liking kids
2. Showing up on time, having equipment
3. Knowing how to operate the machine
4. Following directions
5. Knowledge of bike parts, careful attention to detail
6. Listening to instructions, showing up on time
7. Typing accurately
8. Knowing locations of houses or knowing how to use a GPS

9. Having equipment, knowing a weed from a flower
10. Being polite, listening to orders, making suggestions
11. Following instructions, paying attention to safety rules for frying
12. Knowing the alphabet, paying attention to details

Questions: 1. When working on a job, why is it important to have job skills as well as social skills? 2. How can using social skills help someone acquire job skills?

Worksheet 131: Developing Good Work Habits

The student is to determine which characters on the worksheet are demonstrating good work habits and which social skills they have developed.

Answers may vary.

Answer Key:

1. Yes; making a good first impression; making others feel comfortable
2. No; needs to be more organized, plan ahead
3. No; needs to make a better decision
4. Yes; knowing expectations, extra effort toward excellence
5. No; impolite, not dealing with complaining customer very well
6. No; needs to make a better impression
7. Yes; taking initiative, using common sense
8. Yes; negotiating or compromising

Questions: 1. How does having good work habits affect the people you work with (supervisor, coworkers)? 2. How does having good work habits affect the people you serve (customers, clients)?

Worksheet 132: Following Instructions

The student is to read instructions on the worksheet that might be given to a worker on the job. What problems might occur if the instructions are not followed?

Answer Key:

1. It could be hard to make change, unsafe to take large bills.
2. Someone might steal.
3. The boss won't consider an incomplete application.
4. You might pass on germs.
5. A child could get hit by a car.
6. You could get behind in your work.
7. Your car might get towed.
8. Customers will appreciate the sale, especially if you call attention to sale items.
9. You will know what problems the customers are having.
10. The manager or accountant needs to balance the day's transactions.

Worksheet 133: Dealing with Complaining Customers

The student is to determine what social skills the characters used to handle complaining customers.
Answer Key:

1. Negotiating or compromising
2. Being flexible, making good decisions
3. Understanding another's point of view
4. Knowing expectations, compromising
5. Controlling my emotions
6. Understanding another's point of view, making others feel comfortable

Questions: 1. Have you ever been a complaining customer? How were you treated? 2. Sometimes the problem is not the fault of the person who is taking the complaint. Why is it important to still be polite to that customer? 3. How did the characters try to fix each situation? Do you think they were successful?

Worksheet 134: Being Resourceful

Susanna had to take over for a coworker for a day. The student is to write how Susanna demonstrated being resourceful.
Answer Key:

1. Prioritizes 2. Is organized 3. Takes initiative 4. Has the ability to assess difficulty of tasks 5. Performed so well all day with her tasks that her boss noted her resourcefulness

Questions: 1. How would you describe Susanna in one or two words? 2. Do you think being resourceful is something a person could learn on the job by gaining experience? Explain.

Worksheet 135: Taking Initiative for Promotion

The student is to read over the list of some ways that they could try to get a promotion or better job. Students are then to write some additional ideas.

Answer Key (Examples): Keep up a résumé of your skills and jobs, check the classifieds in your newspaper or online, be available for overtime or extra projects, be pleasant to everyone, make sure you know and use other people's names, make sure people know your name, post successful business or community activities on Facebook (if appropriate), collect letters of character and/or recommendation from people you have worked for, find out what promotions are available at your current job and express interest to supervisors.

Worksheet 136: Dealing with Sick Days

Each situation on this worksheet considers a character who is thinking about using a sick day. The student is to circle Yes or No to indicate whether or not the character should call in sick. *Note:* there are legitimate reasons to call in sick; that is what sick days are for!

Answers may vary if more information is needed.

Answer Key:

1. No; she should go in to work if she is not really sick.
2. Yes; he will not get better if he goes in to work and might be contagious; a fever is a legitimate reason to call in sick.
3. Yes; lice are contagious.
4. No; he is only a little bit late, and it sounds as if the boss really needs help.
5. No; unless her headache is really bad, she can probably treat it with an aspirin. More information is needed to determine how severe the headache is.
6. No; Rico can probably make it to work and has the added incentive of the bonus.

Questions: 1. Why is it important to establish good attendance at whatever job you have? 2. What are some reasons why you should *not* go to work? 3. If someone feels slightly ill, what would they have to consider before deciding whether or not to go in to work?

Worksheet 137: When Your Boss Is Wrong

Students are to read each situation in which the boss has made a mistake and discuss what the character could do.
Answer Key:
1. Hold up the fish food and explain the fish were already fed. 2. Show the leader the order and ask if you could double-check it together. 3. Ask if you could make a sign that clearly shows the correct prices. 4. Show your boss your time card or sign-in sheet that shows the hours you worked. 5. Apologize and explain that you were pretty sure he said 5 p.m. because you knew you had an appointment at 4 p.m., but this may not be worth arguing about. Next time enter the time change requested on your phone or calendar and confirm with the boss.

Name____ Date______________

Worksheet 127

Getting Along with Your Supervisor

What social skills might be helpful in dealing with the following situations at work?

1. Your supervisor just made out the work schedule for the week and got your hours all mixed up. You thought you had told him when you were available, but maybe he didn't hear or understand you. The whole schedule will have to be redone.

____

____

You press
that key there.
And then you hit that twice.
If the screen goes blank,
go back to File-Delete-Return,
Return then Control plus
the F key. Got it?
Sure.

2. You have a new supervisor on your job. He doesn't really know what everyone is supposed to be doing yet, and you realize that he is making some mistakes on orders.

____

____

3. Your supervisor wants you to learn how to do a new task on the computer. She isn't explaining things very well to you, and you aren't sure that you are interested in learning this anyway—but you want to keep your job!

____

____

4. Mornings seem to be a bad time for everyone at your workplace, but especially your boss. She arrives in a very bad mood every morning, which makes everyone else fearful and unsure.

____

____

Getting Along with Your Supervisor (continued)

5. There is going to be an inspection at your workplace tomorrow so your supervisor wants everything to be in really good shape. He asks you to stay late to help get things ready, which matters because you had other plans for tonight.

   ____

   ____

6. No one at work seems to like the supervisor. In fact, some of the employees are planning to call in sick on the same day so that he will have a really hard time getting through the day. You know about it, but aren't sure if you want to be a part of it.

   ____

   ____

Name____________________ Date__________

Worksheet 128

Getting Along with Coworkers

What social skills might help each of the following people get along with the people they have to work with?

1. Can someone change shifts with me? I've got a huge term paper due next week and could really use the extra time to study.

2. I think Gina is picking up your tips from the tables you're waiting on.

3. Someone should talk to Theo about getting to work on time. He's late every morning and we have to get the breakfast orders out!

4. Amy is really nice to work with, but she doesn't do a very good job. I have to go over everything she does and re-do it.

5. Everyone has to do their share and then some, because it's going to be a busy party tonight. Don't wait to be told what to do—if you see something that needs to be done, do it!

6. We can get a raise after six months if we are doing a good job. We can help each other look good!

Name______________________________ Date__________

Worksheet 129

Is This the Right Job for You?

What problems do you see with these characters and the jobs they are doing?

1.

I like getting cash for babysitting, but these kids! They are so loud and they won't do anything I ask. They want me to PLAY with them! I was hoping I could just read a book. I don't even like kids.

2.

Working at a dude ranch is fun because I get to be outdoors. But horses are so big! They really scare me! STAY AWAY!

Is This the Right Job for You? (continued)

3.

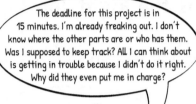

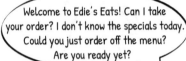

The deadline for this project is in 15 minutes. I'm already freaking out. I don't know where the other parts are or who has them. Was I supposed to keep track? All I can think about is getting in trouble because I didn't do it right. Why did they even put me in charge?

4.

Welcome to Edie's Eats! Can I take your order? I don't know the specials today. Could you just order off the menu? Are you ready yet?

5.

I'm so bored!! I cannot stand putting these little pieces together for hours and hours every day. I want to work somewhere that lets me move around and listen to music.

Name ________________________________ Date ____________

Worksheet 130

Understanding the Skills Required for the Job

What skills might be required in order to perform the following jobs well?

1. Babysitting for three small children ____________________
2. Mowing lawns in your neighborhood ____________________
3. Working the cash register at a hardware store ____________________
4. Making a pizza ____________________
5. Repairing bicycles ____________________
6. Caring for your neighbor's pets while she is on vacation ____________________
7. Entering data into a computer ____________________
8. Delivering flowers ____________________
9. Weeding a garden ____________________
10. Serving at a restaurant ____________________
11. Making French fries ____________________
12. Filing business cards in alphabetical order ____________________

Name____ Date______________

Worksheet 131

Developing Good Work Habits

Which of these characters are demonstrating good work habits? What social skills have they developed?

1.

Good morning, welcome to Frank's Restaurant. May I help you find a place to sit? Would you like to be by a window?

____

____

2.

Sorry I'm late. My car was out of gas again.

____

____

3.

Come on—leave work early and go out with us!
Okay, I'll tell the boss I'm feeling sick. Count me in!

____

____

4.

Well, my work station is all clean and organized now. The next person shouldn't have any trouble finding anything.

____

____

5.

What do you mean, you ordered LARGE fries? You did not. Take these.

____

____

6.

I wore this shirt yesterday, but I think it's still okay to wear to work today.

____

____

7.

Ooh—this window is filthy! I'll get some rags and take care of it.

____

____

8.

I'm sorry, Mr. Jones, but I have another orthodontist appointment on Friday so I'll have to leave early. However, I'll be more than happy to work this weekend or put in extra hours when you need somebody on another day...

____

____

Name________________________________ Date____________

Worksheet 132

Following Instructions

Read the following instructions that might be given while someone is on the job. What problems might occur if they are not followed?

Yeah?
And then what did he say?
Well, you know what I think!?
Blah... blah... blah...

1. Don't take any bills over $20. ________________
2. Lock the safe at 11 p.m. ________________
3. Fill out names and addresses completely for people whom you are using as references on your job application. ________________
4. Wash your hands before handling food. ________________
5. Don't let children cross the street except at the light. ________________
6. No personal phone calls are allowed while working. ________________
7. Employees should park only in special parking areas. ________________
8. All merchandise with a red tag on it is 50% off today. ________________
9. Ask all customers to fill out comment cards or give online review. ________________
10. Turn in all your receipts each evening before you leave. ________________

Name________________________________ Date______________

Worksheet 133

Dealing with Complaining Customers

What social skill(s) did the following characters use to handle customers with complaints?

1.
This food is cold! Take it back!
How about if I make sure you get a free dessert to make up for this?
2.
This model is missing some parts.
That's really unusual! Our company stands behind its products and sales. We'll make it right, don't worry.
3.
I don't like the color of this watch band. It's really awful.
You know, red is not my favorite color either. I can understand why you don't like it.
4.
I have been waiting in line for 15 minutes! Everyone is moving too slowly!
I want to scream.
Well, I am sorry about your wait. There are a lot of people here. I'll work as quickly as I can!
5.
You were late to my house to take the dogs out.
Well, you told me 8 a.m. and that's what time I got there. Perhaps I should come at 7:30 tomorrow instead...?
6.
This soda doesn't have any fizz in it! Your machines must be defective. Don't you ever check them?
I'm sorry it doesn't taste right. I'll replace it with another drink and I'll let my supervisor know about the problem.

1. ______________________
2. ______________________
3. ______________________
4. ______________________
5. ______________________
6. ______________________

Name ____ Date ______________

Worksheet 134

Being Resourceful

Susanna found out that her work partner called in sick, and she suddenly had to do other jobs. How does Susanna demonstrate her resourcefulness?

1. 8:30 a.m. She is pulled off her regular job and has to fill in for someone else.

   ____

   ____

   ____

I'll put everything on my desk aside that isn't urgent and I'll get to it when I can.

2. 9:00 a.m. A customer calls in with a complaint that she knows nothing about.

   ____

   ____

   ____

I'm really sorry about this—it seems to be a big mix-up. I'll take all of the information and make sure I get it to a supervisor. I'll do the best I can to try to get this straightened out.

3. 11:30 a.m. She has to go late to lunch to help clean up a workstation.

   ____

   ____

   ____

Yuck! This hasn't been dusted in weeks! What a mess! Oh well! I'll try to figure out what goes where...

4. 1:00 p.m. After returning from lunch, Susanna finds out there are lots more problems to solve!

   ____

   ____

   ____

This is the pile of things that will have to go to a supervisor; this is the pile of things I think I can handle; and this is the pile of things I think should be thrown out but I'm not the one to do it!

5. 5:00 p.m. Susanna gets ready to leave.

   ____

   ____

   ____

Will Amy be back tomorrow? Please say YES!

Actually, the boss noticed how well you handled everything today and wants to keep you in this department!

Name________________________________ Date____________

Worksheet 135

Taking Initiative for Promotion

Here are some ways you can try to get a promotion or a better job.

Positions
Open
1.
2.
3.
Positions
Open

- Find out what other jobs are available.
- Find out what the qualifications are for other jobs.
- Talk to people in the business who would know about other jobs.
- Be sure to get the best personal evaluation for the present job.
- Let your boss know you are interested in taking on new responsibilities.
- Let your boss know you would like to apply for a different job.
- Have good reasons for why you should be considered for a promotion.
- Maintain a good work record at your present job.
- Look for opportunities to learn new skills and get more training.
- Work on having very good social skills!

Taking Initiative for Promotion (continued)

Can you list some other ways to take initiative for promotion?

1. ____

____

2. ____

____

3. ____

____

4. ____

____

5. ____

____

Name____ Date________________

Worksheet 136

Dealing with Sick Days

Read each of the following situations. Which of the characters do you think should call in sick? Discuss why or why not.

Situation 1
Aya is supposed to work the evening shift at the restaurant. It begins at 6, but she just got a call from a friend to go to a movie. She would rather go to the movie than work. Should she use a sick day?

Yes No

Situation 2
Jimmie has a temperature of 102. He is having trouble breathing and has thrown up a few times. He works at a car wash and knows that they are shorthanded today. Should he use a sick day?

Yes No

Situation 3
Tara works at a school as a teacher's helper. She just got checked for lice and yes—she's got them! Should she use a sick day?

Yes No

Situation 4
Arno is helping paint walls inside a new apartment. His boss needs a second person to help with the trim. Arno overslept, and he is now an hour late. Should he use a sick day?

Yes No

Dealing with Sick Days (continued)

Situation 5
Candice has a slight headache from stress. She knows that her boss is not going to be at work today, but there is a lot of work that she could do without the boss there. Should she use a sick day?

Yes No

Situation 6
Rico hurt his hand in a baseball game last night, and it hurts, but he thinks that taking some aspirin will help. He found out that he will get a $25 bonus if he has perfect attendance for the month. Should he use a sick day?

Yes No

Name______________________________ Date__________

Worksheet 137

When Your Boss Is Wrong

Students are to read each situation in which the boss has made a mistake and discuss what the character could do.

1. You work in a pet store. Your boss told you to feed the fish, but you know that they have already been fed. Overfeeding them might kill them.
2. You are supposed to deliver boxes of cookies to everyone who ordered them on your street. The group leader counted the number of boxes incorrectly, and your order is all messed up.
3. You are collecting money at the school basketball game. The refreshment leader told you the wrong prices for popcorn and soda. People are becoming upset that you are charging too much for food.
4. Your boss handed you your paycheck for the week, but he forgot that you worked overtime on Monday. Your check is written for the wrong amount.
5. Your boss told you to come in to work on Friday at 5 p.m., so you come in at 5 p.m. He is angry because he thought he told you to come in at 4 p.m. and thinks you are late.

Chapter 9

Using Social Skills with Peers

INSTRUCTOR PAGES

Introduction: A peer group consists of individuals who have something in common. This is typically a group that is close in age, similar in social status, or linked by common interests. Most students have a peer group made up of friends at school, in the neighborhood, or in other places in the community. Students might become part of a group by joining a club or participating in a sport. Whatever the composition of the group, its members have to get along. This series of worksheets presents the learner with situations in which they can practice identifying and applying social skills previously taught.

Note: Answers to the worksheets will vary according to the age and developmental stage of your students. The answers provided in the answer keys are models for typical responses you should expect from your students. As with any other activity, accept answers that can be logically supported by facts.

Worksheet 138: Is This a Good Friend?

Students are to read the descriptions of friends and circle their responses to indicate if they agree or not. The heart of this worksheet is in the discussion that should follow. What definition or descriptions can students come up with that define or describe a friend?

Answers may vary.

Answer Key:

1. False—who is ever always in a good mood?
2. True
3. True
4. False—things change
5. True—or at least tries to understand!
6. Answers may vary—what is good advice?
7. True—but explain what "being there" means to you
8. False—but circumstances may affect this

9. False—this is a possessive, jealous friendship
10. True most of the time, we hope—but who can listen all the time?
11. False—you may be wrong
12. False—you may ask for something that isn't good for you

Questions: 1. What do you think are the most important qualities of a good friend? 2. Friends can come and go during different periods of your life. Why do you think that is? Can you think of friends who used to be close to you who are no longer an active part of your life?

Worksheet 139: Ways to Make Friends

Students are to read the list of ideas for ways to make friends and add items to the list.

Questions: 1. What are the most natural ways to make friends? 2. Think of your current friends. How did you first become friends?

Worksheet 140: Are You a Good Friend?

Students are to read the situations in which another individual is involved and come up with a response. How understanding, forgiving, or possessive of a friend are they?

Answers may vary.

Answer Key:

1. Introduce Cynthia to several others who will be at the party.
2. Stop lending things.
3. Find other things to do, try to introduce new topics of conversation, talk honestly with her.
4. Meet Mark at neutral places.
5. Invite her to come to your house.
6. Start inviting Tony to join you when you go out with other friends.

Worksheet 141: Why We Want Friends

This worksheet gives examples of why friendship is so important. Students are to match the reasons with the examples.

Answer Key:

1. b (member of the track team)
2. e (the weird hairstyle is accepted by the others)
3. d (they all feel the same way about study time)
4. c (peers can fulfill a friendship role)
5. a (you might try things you wouldn't think of trying on your own)
6. f (being smart is accepted by this group)

Questions: 1. What are the most important reasons to you for wanting friends? 2. Can you add other reasons to the list?

Worksheet 142: Respecting Others as Individuals

The student is given a list of individuals who may be different from them and is to think of a way that they could show respect and get to know these individuals.
Answer Key:

1. Ask questions about their ethnic background.
2. Attend a service (wedding, church meeting, and so on).
3. Learn some sign language.
4. Make an effort to be patient.
5. Don't be critical—find out what they are good at.
6. Treat them as any other friend.
7. Don't call attention to the problem.
8. Don't act unnatural—be yourself.
9. Ask questions about what it was like.
10. Congratulate them.

Worksheet 143: Taking Advantage of Social Opportunities

On this worksheet, the student is to read the conversations between characters and decide how they are taking advantage of social opportunities that have come up.
Answer Key:

1. Responding to an invitation 2. Helping make phone calls 3. Meeting someone in the store 4. Discussing the dog 5. Joining a class 6. Having a mutual interest in music 7. Sharing a common interest in a movie 8. Taking advantage of opportunity to participate

Questions: 1. Just in the past day or two, what opportunities for social interaction have you noticed? 2. Have you created any social opportunities for others to join?

Worksheet 144: Feeling Outcast

Sometimes students may feel as though they are not accepted in the peer group. On this worksheet, the student is to read the examples of how characters responded to someone being excluded and write their responses.
Answer Key:

1. Offers to join in the existing group, points out her strength 2. Uses creative problem-solving 3. Defends herself 4. Stands up for her friend 5. Goes out of her way to befriend someone else

Questions: 1. Sometimes it's hard to insert yourself into a situation. How did the characters on the worksheet take a positive step? 2. Do you think it's OK to be separate from a group if it's a group you really are not interested in joining?

Worksheet 145: When a Friend Is in Trouble

The student is to identify something that they could do if a friend or peer was experiencing a serious problem such as those on this worksheet.

Answer Key:

1. Talk to him about your concerns.
2. Encourage your friend to stay home and try to work things out.
3. Keep trying to talk to her.
4. Go with him to talk to the parents.
5. Talk to your parents about how they made you feel.
6. Tell your parents that you need their support and understanding.

Questions: 1. Have you encountered any serious problems with friends who have issues? What did you find was the best solution? 2. What would you do if you felt that your friend needed professional help or more help than you could give by just listening or giving advice?

Worksheet 146: Misunderstandings

The student is to decide which social skills might be helpful in clearing up some misunderstandings described on this worksheet and be prepared to discuss their responses.

Answers will vary.

Answer Key:

1. Having a good sense of humor, controlling my emotions
2. Having a good sense of humor, communication skills
3. Having a good work ethic, standing up for myself, negotiating or compromising
4. Controlling my emotions, standing up for myself, communication skills
5. Standing up for myself, controlling my emotions
6. Having a good work ethic, communication skills, negotiating or compromising

Questions: 1. In each case, what exactly was the misunderstanding? How were both parties at fault? 2. Once these misunderstandings have been resolved, do you think the same issue would come up again?

Worksheet 147: Using Social Media Positively

Students are to match examples of using social media with three choices of how it can be used in a positive way.

Answers will vary.

Answer Key:

1. B 2. A 3. C 4. A, B 5. B

Questions: 1. What are some other examples of positive ways you can use social media to connect with others? 2. What are some important causes that you have found that are popular on social media?

Worksheet 148: Types of Bullying

Students are to match examples of bullying with one of the three specific types of bullying listed at the top.
Answer Key:

1. C 2. A 3. A 4. B 5. C 6. B 7. A, B 8. B

Questions: 1. How are these types of bullying hurtful in different ways? 2. Do you have other examples of someone being bullied?

Worksheet 149: Cyberbullying Responses

Students are to discuss how each character in the examples is responding to the cyberbullying situation.
Answer Key:

1. Collecting evidence 2. Not responding at all 3. Using humor to show the bully it didn't hurt 4. Realizing he has supportive friends 5. Ignoring the request for information 6. Reporting the incident to a trusted adult

Questions: 1. How can cyberbulling be worse than bullying in person? 2. What examples can you share from yourself or your friends?

Worksheet 150: Responding to Bullying

Students are to read various strategies for responding to bullying situations and indicate which ones would be most helpful to them.
Answer Key: Answers will vary.

Questions: 1. What are some other helpful techniques for being around bullies and getting them to stop? 2. What is your personal plan for handling a bullying situation? 3. Does your school have a policy in place?

Worksheet 151: Making Friends Online

Students can read about various ways to meet others online with similar interests.

Questions: 1. Have you ever tried any of the examples mentioned to meet others? 2. What are some benefits to having online friendships? 3. What are some drawbacks? 4. What are some safety rules you have put in place to make sure you are in contact with the kind of people who really are seeking friendship?

Name____ Date_______________

Worksheet 138

Is This a Good Friend?

Read the following statements. Circle TRUE if you think it is true or FALSE if you disagree with the statement.

1. A friend is always in a good mood.	**True**	**False**
2. A friend doesn't talk about you behind your back.	**True**	**False**
3. A friend sticks up for you.	**True**	**False**
4. A friend is someone who will always be close to you.	**True**	**False**
5. A friend is someone who understands you and how you think.	**True**	**False**
6. A friend is someone who gives good advice.	**True**	**False**
7. A friend is someone who is always there for you.	**True**	**False**
8. A friend is someone who would lie for you.	**True**	**False**
9. A friend doesn't have other friends—only you.	**True**	**False**
10. A friend is someone who will listen to your problems.	**True**	**False**
11. A friend is someone who agrees with you all the time.	**True**	**False**
12. A friend is someone who would give you whatever you ask.	**True**	**False**

Name____ Date______________

Worksheet 139

Ways to Make Friends

Here are some ideas for ways to make new friends. Can you think of others?

1. Be available.

SKI CLUB
MEETS HERE ON
WEDNESDAYS
AFTER SCHOOL

2. Show your personality.

Have you ever heard Chad tell jokes? He's great!!

3. Be willing to change your opinion about someone.

I didn't know you were interested in horror movies. I know, it doesn't fit my image, does it? But I love to be scared!

4. Make the first move.

I hear you know something about scuba diving.

5. Don't give up—make an effort.

Call Marie
Visit Johnny
Join study group
Invite youth group over.

6. Don't overlook people who seem different than you.

Too old.

Too young.

Wrong gender.

Too loud.

Too rich.

Seems boring.

Name____ Date____________

Worksheet 140

Are You a Good Friend?

What would you do in the following situations? What does your response indicate about how you feel about friendship?

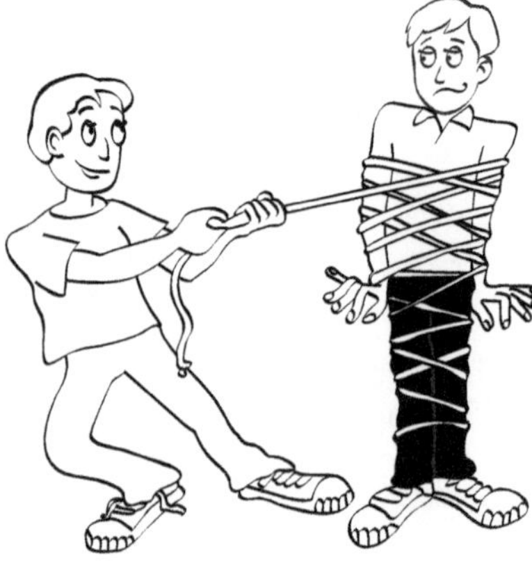

1. Cynthia is very shy and doesn't like parties. You've been invited to a pool party at another friend's house, and you'd really like to go. What can you do about Cynthia?

2. Dennis is always borrowing your stuff—your jean jacket, your softball equipment, and even your car, but when you ask him about borrowing his tennis equipment or a game that he just got, he always seems to have an excuse. What can you do about this?

3. Amanda has her share of problems—divorcing parents, an obnoxious brother, allergies, and constant run-ins with teachers at school. Whenever you call, she wants to go on and on about her problems. At first they seemed important and you didn't mind listening, but now it's like the same story over and over. What can you do?

4. You are really becoming close friends with Mark, a friendly, outgoing guy with a lot of interests—but you can't stand his parents. Whenever you go over to his house, they want to know everything about you, your family, your plans—everything! You'd like to hang out with Mark, but that family is something else!!!

5. Janelle is a terrific artist, and she's willing to give you some tips. It seems, though, that whenever you show up for a lesson, two or three other people are there too, and you are ignored. You'd like to get to know Janelle (not to mention take advantage of the lessons), but her offer always seems to include a lot of other people. What might you do?

6. Tony was a fun friend at first, but now it seems that he doesn't want you to have any other friends. If you hang out with anybody else, he pouts and acts as if you've deserted him. You like Tony, but you'd sure like to have a few other friends too. What will you do?

Name____ Date_______________

Worksheet 141

Why We Want Friends

Why are friends so important to us? Match the reason on the top with the example on the bottom.

__________ 1. Being part of a friendship group gives us an identity.

__________ 2. Being part of a friendship group gives a feeling of safety and acceptance.

__________ 3. There is strength in numbers—when many members of a group make a statement, people listen.

__________ 4. It's nice to have friends or people to do things with.

__________ 5. It can be exciting!

__________ 6. Most people don't want to be thought of as "odd" or singled out for being different.

a.

I'd never skydive by myself--but if we all go --we'll have a blast!

b.

We're on the track team--and we're awesome!

c.

Want to go to a movie on Saturday?
Sure, sounds like fun!

d.

I think we should have more study time.
Me, too!
Let's talk to Mrs. Smith.
OK!

e.

Do you think I ruined my hair?
Hey, you look fine --don't worry about it!
You may start a new fashion trend!

f.

I like being smart!
Me, too! I think school is great!
Want to play some chess?

Name____ Date______________

Worksheet 142

Respecting Others as Individuals

How could you show respect for others in these situations? In what ways could you get to know or understand this person, especially if they are very different from you?

1. Someone whose race is different from yours

____

2. Someone who has different religious beliefs from you

____

3. Someone who has a hearing impairment

____

4. Someone who does not speak your language very well

____

5. Someone who is not a good athlete

____

6. Someone who is very rich

____

7. Someone who stutters

____

8. Someone who is very popular

____

9. Someone who has appeared on television as a model

____

10. Someone who wins awards for academic contests

____

Name____ Date____________

Worksheet 143

Taking Advantage of Social Opportunities

How are these individuals taking advantage of social opportunities that have come up?

1.

Would you like to go to the game with us on Friday?

Oh, sure! Thanks for asking!

____

____

2.

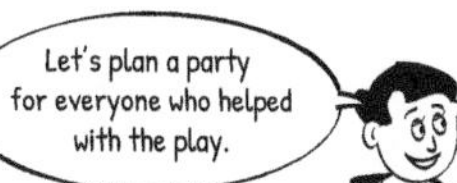
Let's plan a party for everyone who helped with the play.

Yes! I'll help contact everyone to invite them!

____

____

3.

Ketchup ... ketchup ... Hi! Do you happen to know where the ketchup is?

Well, I sure do. Do you shop here often?

____

____

4.

What a pretty dog you have. What kind is it?
She's a husky mix. Do you like dogs?

____

____

5.

Here's the sign-up for people to join an exercise class. It looks like fun.
EXERCISE CLASS
Let's do it.

____

____

6.

I love to listen to music!
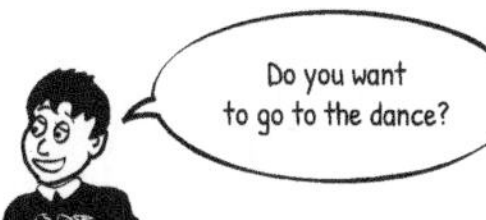
Do you want to go to the dance?

____

____

7.

Hey, we are streaming that really funny movie tonight at my house.

I like that one too. Mind if I watch it with you?

____

____

8.

The hospital is asking for volunteers to help decorate the halls for Christmas.

Let's do it! That might be fun!

____

____

Name ______________________________ Date __________

Worksheet 144

Feeling Outcast

Sometimes you may feel as though everyone is against you or that you are different or not as good as everyone else. How have these individuals attempted to handle those situations?

1.

You seem to have missed out on being assigned to a group.

Hey, I'm ready to work with you on the project. Maybe I could draw some pictures to go with the presentation.

____

2.

Everyone choose a partner for basketball.

Could we be a group of three?

____

3.

Look at that hair—when's the last time you touched it? Or do you have lice again?

If you don't like the way I look or dress, just look at somebody else. Don't you have anything better to do?

____

4.

Get the bug spray—Paula was here.

I really find it offensive when you are so unkind to people. Words can hurt. Someday you will know how it feels. Good-bye.

____

5.

I could go through the entire day and not one person would notice me or say a word to me. I'm sure feeling sorry for myself. There's Amy all by herself at the lunch table.

Hi Amy... Would you like some company?

____

Name________________________________ Date____________

Worksheet 145

When a Friend Is in Trouble

What could you do or say to help a friend if they were in serious trouble or experiencing a problem? Consider the following situations.

1. Your friend has started using some recreational drugs. He doesn't seem to care much about school or even work anymore.

   ____

2. Your friend is having a lot of problems at home since his parents' divorce. In fact, he is thinking about running away or possibly moving in with a relative in another state.

   ____

3. Your friend is being given some bad advice from another friend—but when you try to set her straight, your friend won't believe you. You're frustrated that your friend won't listen to you.

   ____

4. Your friend borrowed his parents' car without permission and put a huge dent in the front of it, got a speeding ticket, and is now afraid to go home.

   ____

5. Your friend is a different race than you, and your parents are not willing to accept her as a guest in their house. You are embarrassed and upset by your parents' behavior, but what can you do? Your friend feels hurt and upset.

   ____

6. Your friend lied to her parents about where she was last night—she said she was with YOU. You know that she will get in a lot of trouble if she's caught in a lie. You also know that her parents will be talking to your parents.

   ____

Name ______________________________ Date ____________

Worksheet 146

Misunderstandings

Which of these social skills might be helpful in clearing up misunderstandings between peers in each of the following situations? Explain how you could use them.

Having a good sense of humor	Having a good work ethic	Using communication skills
Standing up for myself	Controlling my emotions	Negotiating or compromising

Situation 1: You thought your friend wanted to meet at 5 o'clock, and he thought it was 6 o'clock. You have been waiting for an hour and are pretty upset.

Situation 2: You called a friendly greeting to your friend as you passed in the hall, but she didn't look at you or answer you. You are wondering why she is mad at you. Later, she said that she didn't see or hear you.

Situation 3: Every time you work on a project with Alan, he wants to leave early to watch his favorite TV shows. He doesn't seem to mind leaving you with the work.

Situation 4: Your sister had a rough day at work and is angry at you because she says you didn't return her sweater that you borrowed. You do have the sweater, but you put it in a drawer instead of hanging it up in her closet.

Situation 5: You are with a group of friends who want to go to a movie that is violent and starts at midnight. You told your friends that you don't want to go because you have to get up early the next day, but they are teasing you about not wanting to see a violent movie because you are scared.

Situation 6: You are trying to earn money to go on a trip and have saved up $500. A friend of yours wants to know if he can borrow some money to get his car fixed. When you explained that you are saving the money, he said that you were not a very good friend and that he would give you money if you needed it.

Name____ Date______________

Worksheet 147

Using Social Media Positively

How do these examples show how social media can be used in a positive way?

A. Expressing yourself B. Connecting to friends C. Supporting causes

1. I'm going to send this TikTok video to Shalimar. She'll think it's really funny!

2. I just posted my latest art project on Instagram. I'm really proud of myself!

3. Wow! The animal shelter just took in 15 abandoned dogs! They are fundraising to get help!

4. I just took a black-and-white video of the birds in the park. I think it's artsy and cool. I'm going to add music and show it to my art class.

5. Colin just posted a hilarious video of when we were kids bouncing on his trampoline. I'm going to share it with my friends on Facebook.

Name________________________________ Date____________

Worksheet 148

Types of Bullying

Bullying is when a person demonstrates unwanted or aggressive behavior toward another. Which of the examples below show these types of bullying?

A – Verbal B – Social C – Physical

1. Spitting on someone
2. Teasing someone
3. Calling someone names
4. Ruining someone's reputation
5. Tripping someone
6. Spreading rumors online
7. Threatening to tell lies
8. Leaving someone out on purpose

Name______________________________ Date__________

Worksheet 149

Cyberbullying Responses

Cyberbullying uses social media to intimidate others. How is each character below responding to the cyberbullying?

1.

Oh my goodness! That bully has posted all kinds of nasty things about me. I'm taking a screen shot of this and letting her know.

2.

Well, the bully has made fun of my hair again. Delete, delete, delete. Not worth responding.

3.

I really don't know why that bully posted an embarrassing picture of me online. I'm going to make a humorous comment about it. It won't get to me.

4.

The bully has posted threats to hurt me. I see that ten of my friends have responded to him by saying they will be right there with me.

Cyberbullying Responses (continued)

5.

I don't recognize the screen name of this person who wants to know all about me. I'm not going to give out any information. I think it might be my bully under a fake name.

6.

At first this was just annoying, but I'm going to report this to my parents and maybe my school counselor. I think this bully is intimidating other kids as well.

Name____ Date____________

Worksheet 150

Responding to Bullying

Here are some strategies for responding to people who bully. Mark the ones that you think would be helpful or interesting for you to try.

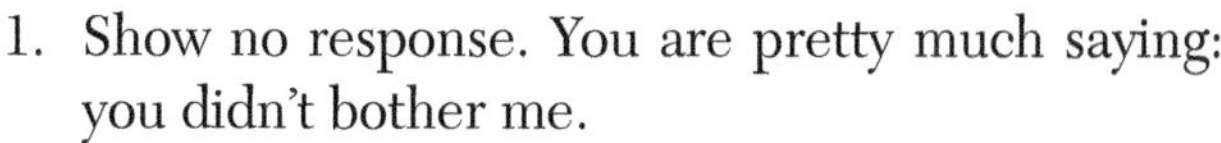

1. Show no response. You are pretty much saying: you didn't bother me.
2. Keep your emotions under control. Don't get drawn into a situation that could make things worse. Deep breaths.
3. Use humor. If insulted, laugh it off or show a puzzled face to show that you prefer to laugh at the situation. It's so ridiculous you can't even take it seriously.
4. Remove yourself. Walk away, walk away, walk away.
5. Tell someone. You are not at fault; your feelings are worthwhile. Share how you are feeling about the situation with a trusted friend or adult. Even if you don't want them to act on your behalf, you have documented the incident by talking (or writing in a journal).
6. Avoid danger zones. You might want to walk down a different hallway, sit at a new lunch table, or make sure you have a friend with you if you are getting on the bus. You wouldn't want to fall into a hole on purpose; go around it.
7. Have a comeback line ready for the bully: "Do you feel better now? Did that just make your day? Sorry, can't stay for the entertainment."
8. Don't be a bystander if you see someone being bullied. If everyone took a stand against bullying, it would stop. Bullies want attention and power and they need an audience to keep going. Turn that audience into bystanders who will make a difference. Be the first one if you have to. Say: "Knock it off. No one thinks that's cool. Be a better human."

Name____ Date______________

Worksheet 151

Making Friends Online

Thanks to technology, there are many ways to meet others with similar interests and join in virtual relationships. Here are some ideas.

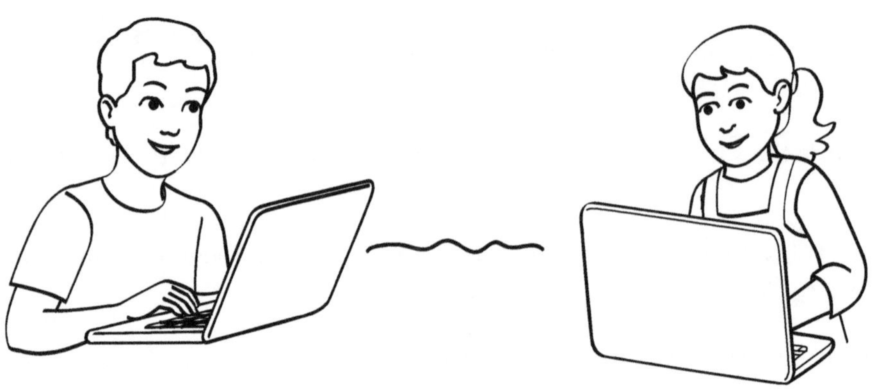

1. Investigate friendship apps. Check out apps such as spot-a-friend, meetup, making authentic friendships (for persons with ADHD, autism), Ablo.live (connecting with people from other countries), friender, bumble BFF, and others. Be sure to find out if there are subscription costs.

2. Participate in social media comments. Leave positive comments or interesting questions on posts from others; ask for more information, encourage the poster, or share your enthusiasm.

3. Join online groups that focus on a particular interest that you may have, for example, dog (Meet My Dog), music (Tastebuds), bird watching (I Bird Pro), fashion design (Autodesk Sketchbook), and so on. Follow the comments or blogs to get to know some people. Some groups have a local feature in which you can arrange to meet up in person to join an activity (bike riding, visit a museum, and so on).

4. Take an online class for fun! Using Zoom or other platforms, you can interact with others on a virtual visit to another country, write a screenplay, listen to historical talks, participate in games, cook a meal, and discover so many other activities that can be shared with others.

Chapter 10

Using Social Skills in the Community

INSTRUCTOR PAGES

Introduction: We are all members of some sort of larger social group based on where we live or our common interests. People need to interact with neighbors, community helpers, and others who live in the same general area. There are many things that community groups have in common. They share the same schools, shopping centers, parks and playgrounds, and community opportunities. The community leadership affects everyone in that area. Individuals can become good citizens by respecting the people who live near them as well as by respecting community ordinances and participating in community events. It is very important for students to view themselves as positive members of their community with something to contribute.

Note: Answers to the worksheets will vary according to the age and developmental stage of your students. The answers provided in the answer keys are models for typical responses you should expect from your students. As with any other activity, accept answers that can be logically supported by facts or the student's particular situation.

Worksheet 152: Respecting the Property of Others

Students are to put a check mark by the examples that show an individual respecting the property of others.
Answer Key:

1. No 2. No 3. No 4. Yes 5. No 6. Yes

Questions: 1. What evidence do you see of disrespect toward property as you travel through your community? 2. What efforts have been made to improve property eyesores?

Worksheet 153: Demonstrating Good Manners Toward Others

Students are to discuss how the characters on the worksheet are showing good manners toward others. They should write some social skills that are demonstrated.

Answer Key:

1. Understanding another's point of view, being a good listener
2. Having a good sense of humor, being flexible
3. Controlling emotions, making a first impression

Worksheet 154: Respecting Community Authority Figures

When you are in the community, you might find yourself in a situation in which you interact with an authority figure. Students are to write how they could respond to authority figures in the situations on the worksheet.

Answer Key:

1. Be polite, listen. 2. Pay the fine. 3. Practice. 4. Move on, talk somewhere else. 5. Discuss it politely with her, possibly negotiate. 6. Go into the store with only one friend, skip the store and go somewhere else. 7. Don't argue if you don't have the identification, be polite. 8. Talk to your parents for permission.

Worksheet 155: Being Aware of Local Issues

The student is to find out what is going on in the local community by reading or listening to local media. Examples are provided on the worksheet.

Answers will vary.

Questions: 1. What forms of media are most helpful in spreading news about the community? 2. What types of public meetings are held regularly that also involve local concerns?

Worksheet 156: Supporting Efforts to Improve the Community

The student is to identify some community improvements that are going on or being considered in their community. How can someone get involved? Examples are provided on the worksheet.

Answers will vary.

Worksheet 157: Dealing with Unhelpful People

Students are to write how they might respond to a person who is not willing to listen to the character's idea or problem with a community situation.

Answer Key:

1. Estimate costs, get a petition, put ad in the local paper.
2. Find out places where dogs are welcome, investigate operating a dog park.
3. Ask for designated picnic areas, picnic table reservations.
4. Complain to the manager of the theater.

5. Put up signs, ask for police patrol periodically through area, initiate clean-up days.
6. Find out from local authority person who has priority on a path and if a path is wide enough to be shared.

Questions: 1. How were some of the people on the worksheet being unhelpful or even rude? 2. How can you find out what person or agency would be able to help make changes in the community if you had a specific idea or problem?

Worksheet 158: Helping in Your Community

The student is to list community service organizations in their community and give examples of how someone could get involved in service.

Answer Key:

1. Volunteer to tutor. 2. Join Big Brothers/Big Sisters. 3. Offer to rake the yard. 4. Offer to help with shopping. 5. Find out what errands are needed, locate community drivers who provide this service. 6. Grab a friend and go visit! 7. Join a community choir and visit nursing homes; adopt a grandparent. 8. Offer to babysit or take the children to a park or zoo (with permission). 9. Help paint a sign to be displayed at the town square. 10. Make signs, help collect the cans.

Questions: 1. What is necessary to get involved in a community service group? 2. What could you or you and some friends do on your own to help other needy people in your community?

Worksheet 159: Showing Respect to Older People

The student is to discuss how the characters on the worksheet are showing respect to people who are older than they are.

Answers may vary.

Answer Key:

1. Giving up a seat on the bus 2. Letting an older person go ahead of you in the check-out line 3. Being aware that you may be making noise or playing in an area close to the older couple 4. Offering to pick up something 5. Being respectful to a veteran 6. Offering to help an older person with some new technology

Questions: 1. How does it show consideration when you ask people if you could do something for them, even if they say no, thank you? 2. Do you think some older people might be offended if you try to do something for them? 3. Who are older people in your life whom you would like to see treated well by others?

Worksheet 160: Welcoming Visitors to Your Community

What would visitors want to see in your community? Students are to design a brochure that includes highlights. The worksheet lists some ideas.

Answers will vary.

Name________________________________ Date____________

Worksheet 152

Respecting the Property of Others

Check which of these individuals are being good neighbors by showing respect for the property of others.

1.
Let's carve our names in this tree!
Hey, I've got a better idea. Let's spray paint them on this wall!!
2.
It's a shortcut to get to the library by cutting across this yard. See? There's already a path. Everyone else does it.
3.
Are you done with that soda? Just toss the cup out the window. One little piece of trash won't matter.
4.
It's a real pain to have to carry a little shovel and bag whenever I take Sweetie for a walk. But I guess it could be a problem.
5.
Let's ride our mountain bikes up the Martinsons' hill. They won't care.
6.
I wonder if we could play softball in the field next to that huge house. Why don't we ask them first?

Name______________________________ Date__________

Worksheet 153

Demonstrating Good Manners Toward Others

Discuss how these people are showing good manners toward others. Write the social skills they are demonstrating.

1. ____________________

2. ____________________

3. ____________________

Good morning, Mrs. Beason. How are you today?
Well, I've got aches and pains all over. My corns and bunions just aren't getting any better. It's awful to be old.
I'm sorry to hear that. Let me know if there's anything I can do for you!
Boys, your music is just too loud! We can hardly hear ourselves talk at the dinner table.
Oh, sorry about that. We'll try to keep it down.
Thanks. We'd really appreciate it.
No problem. But remember—someday we may be famous musicians and then you'll have to PAY to hear us. Now it's free.
I can wait.
This guy is driving so fast, he's practically in my back seat!
Give him the finger! He shouldn't be on the road!
Wait a minute—I think it's my uncle. He's probaly late for his doctor's visit. I'll pull over so he can pass. I'm not in that big of a hurry.

Name________________________________ Date______________

Worksheet 154

Respecting Community Authority Figures

How could you respond appropriately to the authority figures in the situations below?

stop
BE ON
TIME

1. A police officer who pulls you over for running through a stop sign

____

2. The librarian who informs you that your book is overdue and you now have a huge fine to pay

____

3. The driver's education instructor who tells you that your parallel parking is awful and that you aren't going to get your license until it improves

____

4. The principal of an elementary school who says that you and your group of friends need to keep moving when you go past the school, not stand in front and talk, because parents are coming by with cars to pick up their little kids

____

5. The manager of a restaurant who doesn't want you and your friends skateboarding, in-line skating, or bike riding in his wonderfully smooth parking lot—even after the store is closed!

____

6. The security guard at the mall who says that only two teenagers are allowed in the stores at a time

____

7. The bank teller who says you have to show proof of identification to cash a check, even though you have had a checking account at the bank for six months

____

8. The manager of a tanning booth who won't let you tan unless you are over 16 years of age or are there with a parent

____

Name________________________________ Date____________

Worksheet 155

Being Aware of Local Issues

Find out what is going on in your community that concerns you, your peers, your family, and other aspects of your life. Check through your local media sources, including TV, radio, and online information. What's important in your community that you need to be aware of? Here are some possibilities:

- Recreational places for teens to visit
- Rules and regulations for using the beach facilities
- Restoring or destroying historic buildings
- School policies for graduation
- Youth employment procedures and opportunities
- Prices going up at the local retail stores
- Community lessons or sports events
- Businesses going on strike
- Remodeling schools in the community
- Road repair

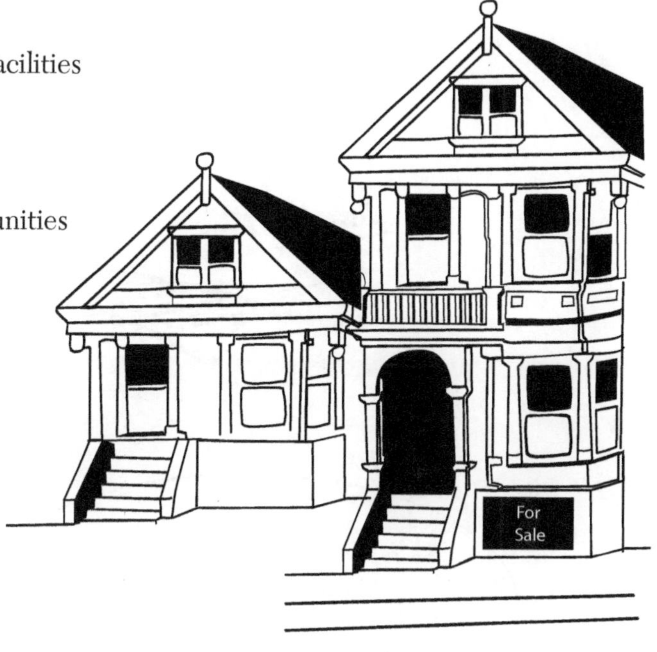
For
Sale

List some other possibilities:

____

____

____

____

____

____

____

____

____

____

____

____

Name ________________________________ Date ____________

Worksheet 156

Supporting Efforts to Improve the Community

What are some ways you can become involved in your community? Here are some possibilities. On the back of this sheet, list some other possibilities.

1.

We need a railroad crossing sign and lights at the highway. There have been too many accidents there.

2.

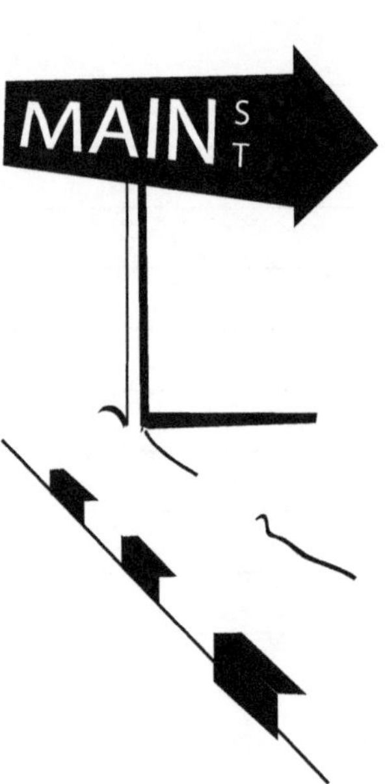
We're having a Cruise Night this summer in July. We're asking everyone to clear the main route through town for a few hours so the old cars can go through on parade.
MAIN ST

Supporting Efforts to Improve the Community (continued)

3.

4.

5.

The speed limit in front of the school is not being followed by anyone. Drivers are going too fast down that road. We need to post a lower limit. I know this will be unpopular, but we've got a lot of little kids who walk to school.
SCHOOL
The new mall just opened. I try to do my shopping locally to give my business to the local merchants.
If we want this beach to stay open, we need to make sure we follow the rules. No littering, stay within the ropes, etc. Hey...I wonder if we could add a snack bar!

Name________________________________ Date______________

Worksheet 157

Dealing with Unhelpful People

How could someone respond to the people below who are not being helpful?

1. Talking to a city official about an idea

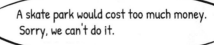

A skate park would cost too much money.
Sorry, we can't do it.

2. Being corrected by a neighbor

No dogs here. Find another spot.
NO DOGS

3. Moved aside by a pushy person

We want this picnic table.
We always sit there.

Dealing with Unhelpful People (continued)

4. Not allowed to go into theater

You just told those people that the movie was sold out, but you let those guys in.
Sold out
Well, they are friends of mine.

5. Not given helpful information when asked

I'm supposed to pick up some forms. Can you help me?
Sorry, just look through all this and see if you can figure it out.

6. Using a shared access path

This is a bike path! Get out of the way!
Hey, walkers can come here, too! Be careful and slow down!

Name____ Date________________

Worksheet 158

Helping in Your Community

Can you list 10–15 community agencies that help people in need in the area where you live? What are some ways that you could get involved in helping others by volunteering your time, money, or talents?

Here are some examples to get you started:

Library Tutors for Reading
Habitat for Humanity
YMCA
Meals on Wheels

How could you help in these situations?

1. A child who has difficulty reading
2. A child who would benefit from an older teen spending time with them
3. An older person who cannot rake leaves in their yard
4. A person who broke her ankle and cannot easily get to the store
5. A neighbor who cannot drive any longer
6. People in a nursing home who have no visitors
7. People who are lonely
8. A busy single mom who needs an occasional babysitter
9. A community play that would like to have its performance dates advertised
10. A food drive for canned goods

Name____ Date______________

Worksheet 159

Showing Respect to Older People

How are these characters showing respect to people who are older than they are?

1.

This bus is crowded. Go ahead and take my seat. You have a lot to carry.

2.

Don't push. Let Mrs. Jones go first to check out. We are not in a hurry.
Cheese
Bread
Pizza
Chicken
Soup

Showing Respect to Older People (continued)

3.
Good afternoon, Mr. and Mrs. McDermott. Hope you're having a pleasant evening. We'll try not to break any windows! Ha, ha, just kidding.
4.
I'm going to the concession stand. Would you like me to get something for you?

Showing Respect to Older People (continued)

5.
I can see that you are a veteran. My dad served, too. Thank you for your service to our country.
ARMY
6.
You are pretty good with your smartphone. Would you like me to show you some apps that I'm using? I bet you would like them.

Name____ Date______________

Worksheet 160

Welcoming Visitors to Your Community

What would visitors want to see in your community? Design a brochure that includes the important sites, events, and interesting things about where you live.

Ideas . . .

What are some places where people would want to go?

Where do people like to eat?

What are some interesting things to see?

Is there a local museum?

Is there a zoo?

What events does your community have?

Does your community do anything special for holidays?

Do you have a parade for certain events?

VISIT
BEAUTIFUL
SMITHVILLE !

Chapter 11

Using Social Skills in Leisure Settings

INSTRUCTOR PAGES

Introduction: Most people have time in their day between school, working, and being in the community to engage in activities of their choosing. This might take the form of a hobby, a sport, a particular interest in a topic, or simply engaging in reading, singing, or hanging out with friends. The student might choose to be with other people or indulge in a leisure activity alone. The idea is to encourage students to find, try out, and stick with activities for the purpose of enjoying life.

Note: Answers will vary according to the student's interest, abilities, and opportunities.

Worksheet 161: A Few of Your Favorite Things

Students are to come up with a personal narrative that describes a meaningful activity or place of contentment.

Answers will vary.

Questions: 1. How do you typically spend your leisure time? 2. If you had no restrictions (time, money, availability, and so on) what would you like to do or try? 3. Are there ways to investigate new leisure activities without a lot of up-front cost or commitment?

Worksheet 162: Unwritten Rules

Students will examine examples of activities that usually involve some sort of rule or procedure that is commonly understood. They are to try to figure out what that unwritten rule is.

Answer Key:

1. Don't stay too close together when climbing for safety. 2. Wait until the pianist has completely finished performing before applauding. 3. Keep your dog on a leash in a public place. 4. Don't put your trash on the floor in a theater. 5. Quiet atmosphere is desired when engaged in an activity such as yoga. 6. Don't

yell out when you are supposed to be quietly watching birds. 7. Use common sense to not endanger others using the trampoline. 8. Don't ride a horse until you have the instructions and can comply with them. 9. Don't argue with the umpire during a game. 10. Don't use a skateboard in a crowded place.

Questions: 1. Which of the examples of procedures would most likely have a sign to help users know what to do? 2. Which of the examples could be figured out by using common sense?

Worksheet 163: Inviting Others to Join In

Students are to match the activities that could include others with the choices: personal invitation, open invitation, social media. More than one answer could be appropriate.

Answer Key:

1. A, C 2. A, B 3. A 4. B, C

Questions: 1. Which invitation style appeals most to you? 2. What are the advantages/disadvantages of each method of inviting someone to join in?

Worksheet 164: Dealing with Social Anxiety

Students are to match social activities with a tip that might help them in each example.

Answers may vary.

Answer Key:

1. C (more information) 2. E (go with a friend) 3. A (planned leaving time) 4. D (small step forward) 5. B (comfortable appearance) 6. F (safe spot)

Questions: 1. What type of social activities are hard for you to participate in? 2. What strategies have helped you or seem as though they might be helpful?

Worksheet 165: Special Events

Students are given examples of special social events that might be available to them. They are to list some factors that they should prepare for in each case.

Answers may vary.

Answer Key:

1. Find out leaving time, what to bring, who is going. 2. How much will it cost, transportation? 3. Will the crowds be a problem, how to get involved, how to leave easily? 4. What are the rules for attending, what materials are needed, how many people and dogs will be there? 5. What are the registration procedures and cost, who will be on your team, where is it held? 6. Who is organizing this event, what do you need to bring, what will the weather be like?

Questions: 1. Which of the examples involve getting along socially with others? 2. Which social skills would be helpful in each situation?

Worksheet 166: Popular Leisure Activities for Teens

Students are to indicate which popular activities sound interesting to them, which ones have already been tried, and which ones they would like to attempt. Try to add to the list.

Answers will vary.

Name____ Date______________

Worksheet 161

A Few of Your Favorite Things

What are your personal favorite activities? If you were going to build the happiest place for yourself, what would it consist of? What things/objects, what people, what events would you choose to put in this background or event? It could be a real time/place/event or you could use your imagination.

Here are some examples:

I love sports. Whenever I have the time, I watch my favorite teams (in person if I can get tickets!), and I follow the statistics because I'm a real fan. I'm a decent athlete, but I really enjoy just playing pickup basketball for fun. For me, being active and caring about a team is fun.

When I'm stressed, I like to play my guitar and write songs. I don't really perform for anyone, but I shut my bedroom door or go outside and sit under a tree. Music relaxes me and writing songs is an outlet to express how I'm feeling. Maybe I'll be a rock star someday, but it doesn't really matter!

My best friend and I are involved in dog training. We both have smart dogs (I have a beagle, she has a shepherd mix), and on weekends we go to the local dog park and use the obstacles. The dogs love it! We think we are ready for some competitions. It's a great hobby.

Maybe you'll think I'm a nerd, but I love going to museums and learning about—everything! I'm fascinated by mummies, pyramids, skeletons, jewelry, and the Old West. I could live in a museum and never come out. I read all of the information cards and am fascinated with things that don't exist anymore.

When I have free time, I help my uncle restore an old car. It's a 1972 Chevy Nova street car. He calls it a muscle car. It might take years before it's finished, but when we're done we can take it to car shows and drive it around. I'm learning a lot from my uncle about how to get parts and how to put it all together. I enjoy being with him too because it's something we do together.

Name____ Date______________

Worksheet 162

Unwritten Rules

These students are having fun participating in leisure activities; however, they are not aware of rules or procedures that should be followed. What do they need to know?

1.

I'm going to race you!
Hey, you're in my way!

2.

Yea! Wonderful performance!

Shhh, he isn't finished with the piece yet. It was just a pause between movements. Wait until he takes his hands off the piano before applauding.

Unwritten Rules (continued)

3.
Where did Rex go? Rex! Rex!! Come here, buddy!
4.
I'm finished with all I want of the popcorn. I'll just leave it on the floor by my feet.
5.
Breathe in ....
Where's my phone? I need louder music.

Unwritten Rules (continued)

6.

I think I see a red-headed woodpecker....
HEY! HEY! Let me find my phone so I can take a picture!

7.

Let's see how high we can get your brother to bounce!

Unwritten Rules (continued)

8.

GIDDY UP!!

Wait! I haven't explained how to stop yet!

9.

The ump called you OUT.

I was not out! I was safe!

Unwritten Rules (continued)

10.

I can do all kinds of tricks! Look out, people. I'm coming through!

Name____ Date______________

Worksheet 163

Inviting Others to Join In

Some activities are more fun when others join in. How are these characters inviting others to join in? More than one answer might be correct!

A – Personal invitation   B – Open invitation   C – Social media

1.

TEXT: There's a surprise party for Elin at my house tomorrow at 6. RSVP if you're coming!

2.

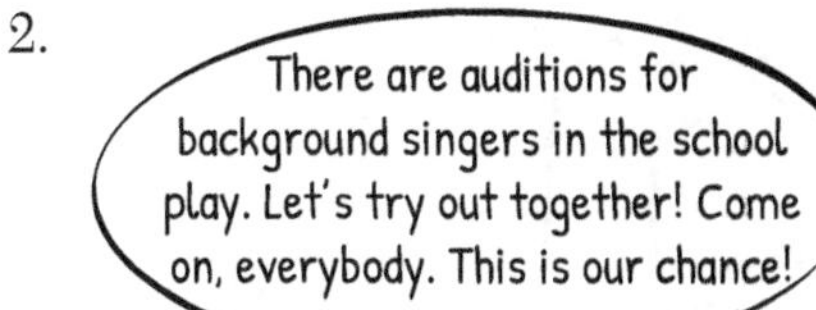
There are auditions for background singers in the school play. Let's try out together! Come on, everybody. This is our chance!

Inviting Others to Join In (continued)

3.

Hey, we are going spelunking. Do you know what that is?
Nope.
We are going to explore a cave. Why don't you come with us?
I don't know anything about it.
No problem. We have maps and all of the equipment. We will see all kinds of rock formations. And it will be cold! Bring a sweatshirt.
Do you think I would like it?
I know you're not afraid of tight spaces and I know you enjoy rocks. I think you would love it.
OK, I'm in.

Inviting Others to Join In (continued)

4.

Instagram: The airport club is featuring some World War II bomber planes like this one on display this weekend. Would anyone like to go? It's not very expensive and they will give guided tours. My dad will drive us there. Comment for more info.

Name____ Date____________

Worksheet 164

Dealing with Social Anxiety

These individuals want to join in social activities, but they are fearful. How are these tips helping them to socialize?

A – Having a planned leaving time
B – Feeling comfortable in your appearance
C – Finding out more about the event/meeting
D – Taking a small step toward joining in
E – Having a friend stay with you
F – Finding a safe spot

1.

I'm supposed to go to a meeting about attending a field trip to our state capitol. I don't want to go to the meeting OR on the field trip, but my parents think I should get involved. I'm not going to commit to the field trip, but I agreed to go to the meeting and get the information. I'll talk it over with my parents later.

2.

Well, my friends and I are going to a party and I'm afraid they'll leave me as soon as we walk in the door. Then I'll be standing around all awkward and regretting every second.

No, Jules, we are sticking together. No one is leaving anyone alone. We are all shy!

Dealing with Social Anxiety (continued)

3.

Why did I agree to have coffee with this person I don't even know? I'll make sure he knows I have an appointment in 40 minutes so I have an escape route already set.

4.

It's hard for me to join in with others, but I'm going to say yes to activities that I haven't tried before. In my mind, I know it's good for me and I'm going to push myself out of my comfort zone a little bit.

Dealing with Social Anxiety (continued)

5.

6.

I'm nervous about volunteering at the food pantry, but I'm wearing my favorite jeans, a very comfortable shirt, and I feel as though I look my best. I'm going to smile, even though I'm unsure of what's going to happen.
There are so many people in the room, but my safe place is going to be that chair near the door. People are coming and going so they can say hi to me or not. I'm going to sit down, cross my legs, try to look relaxed, and just be in the room. It's easier than standing!

Name____ Date______________

Worksheet 165

Special Events

Here are some examples of social events that occur occasionally. What might you have to be aware of ahead of time in order to attend and enjoy these events?

1. Going to an amusement park for a day with a group from your school

____

____

2. Attending a concert at a fairground venue

____

____

Special Events (continued)

3. Participating in a block party in your neighborhood with food trucks, rides for little kids, and table games

____

____

4. Taking your dog to obedience classes

____

____

5. Registering your team for a local triathlon (swimming, biking, running)

____

____

6. Volunteering to clean up hiking trails in organized sections

____

____

Name________________________________ Date____________

Worksheet 166

Popular Leisure Activities for Teens

Which of these activities or places to visit sound interesting to you? Circle ones that you have already tried. Put a * by ones that you would like to try. Feel free to add to the list!

escape room	midnight bowling	scavenger hunt
rock climbing	hiking	geocaching
amusement park	road trip	explore remote places
table/board games	redecorate a room	make a movie
do a TikTok challenge	learn to play guitar	take an online class
visit a museum	visit a zoo	go to a sports event
go to a music festival	go on a nature walk	minigolf
learn a new language	visit a historic site	go white water rafting
visit a state park	start a business	care for animals

Chapter 12

What Others Need to Know

INSTRUCTOR PAGES

Introduction: There are many resources, such as this book, that are directed toward helping struggling individuals develop good social skills so they can find a place in society. But what about increasing awareness on the part of well-adjusted individuals toward welcoming these individuals into society by using their own influence and social success? This involves changing the focus from those who are socially needy to those who are able to help.

The following set of worksheets focuses on teaching other people ways to view and treat individuals who are on the path of learning appropriate social skills. These worksheets give examples of how to treat others with kindness, respect, patience, and using one's own skills and influence to assist others.

What can YOU do to make a difference? Be a model. Don't label or use derogatory words. Stop bullying whenever you have an opportunity. Gently correct when appropriate. Always look for common ground and goodness in others. As a teacher, teach these skills to all of your students. As a student, think about how YOU can help make a difference in someone's life.

Note: Answers will vary according to the student's interests, abilities, and opportunities.

Worksheet 167: Treating Others with Kindness

Students are to indicate which character in each example is demonstrating kindness.

Answer Key:

1. A 2. B 3. B 4. A

Questions: 1. What other examples can you think of for ways to be kind to someone who has difficulty fitting in? 2. Which of these would be hard for you to do?

Worksheet 168: Treating Others with Respect

Students are to match the example of a character treating someone with respect with one of five choices.
Answer Key:

1. C 2. E 3. A 4. D 5. B

Questions: 1. How does each situation show someone being respectful? 2. How could each of these situations go wrong if the individual is not sensitive to the other person?

Worksheet 169: Treating Others with Patience

Students are to give a possible response to how to be patient in a given situation.

Answers may vary.

Answer Key:

1. Redirect the boy to more appropriate behavior. 2. Assure the girl that there is plenty of time to complete the project to make it look good. 3. Give the person an "out"—explain that it is fine to not participate in an uncomfortable discussion. 4. Calm the person down, tell him to relax, practice going over the speech ahead of time. 5. Coach the boy to get his order ready ahead of time.

Questions: 1. How could demonstrating patience be helpful to the individuals who are lacking in social skills? 2. What could be done ahead of time to help the individual in each situation?

Worksheet 170: Sharing Your Skills and Influence

Students are to discuss how the characters in each example are using their own skills and influence to help the socially needy character.
Answer Key:

1. The boy is inviting the other boy to come to his house, wear clothes that show he is part of their group. 2. The girl is stating her position that she will not be a part of bullying; she is using her popularity to suppress bullying among her friends. 3. The girl is including the other girl in a social activity to help her appearance. 4. The boy is preparing the second boy for a social activity by coaching him as to what to wear. 5. The girl is inviting the other girl to join in a class for fun.

Questions: 1. What personality skills do some of the characters have that they are sharing? 2. Some of the characters seem to be leaders or have influence over others. How could this help to benefit someone less social?

Name________________________________ Date____________

Worksheet 167

Treating Others with Kindness

Which of the following characters in each situation is demonstrating kindness toward someone?

Situation 1: Calling Attention to a Problem

A.

Sarah, I can help you with that worksheet. We can work together in the back.

B.

Teacher! Sarah is having trouble with that worksheet! Can you stop the class and explain how to do it again?

Situation 2: Including Others in Social Events

A.

We're all going roller skating on Friday. Pete won't be able to skate, so don't say anything to him about it. Maybe he won't find out.

B.

The whole class is going bowling. Pete probably can't bowl, but I bet he would like to hang out with us and watch.

Treating Others with Kindness (continued)

Situation 3: Keep Forgiving Shortcomings

A.

I can't work with Bob in our group. He talks all the time, and it's so hard to focus!

B.

Bob talks a lot, but I'm going to tell him that this is our time for listening to each other so he has to be quiet but he'll get his turn to talk. We all will get a turn.

Situation 4: Emphasizing a Disability

A.

Ingrid can't help her facial tics. We are used to them by now and we don't really notice them so much.

B.

This is what Ingrid looks like when she gets stressed. It's so funny!

Name______________________________ Date__________

Worksheet 168

Treating Others with Respect

How are these individuals treating someone with respect? Match the response with the situation below.

A. Look for positives B. Listen C. Learn about the disability or situation
D. Don't talk down E. Affirm or agree when you can

1. _______ Zoe has a friend with Asperger's Syndrome. She went online to learn about this condition so that she could understand what it's like for her friend.

2. _______ Brian is very sensitive to loud noises, bright lights, and other environmental stimuli. James wanted to do something with Brian, so he asked him what they could do or where they could go that would make Brian feel comfortable. Brian explained that he likes to go walking early in the morning, so they agreed to meet the next day at the park.

3. _______ Four students were working on a project in a group that included Jade, who is very shy and rarely expresses her opinions. One of the students remarked that Jade was an excellent artist and maybe she would like to sketch some of the group's ideas. Jade nodded and said, "I do like to draw. I can do that!"

4. _______ Raymond was talking to some kids about how he knew all about helicopters. Frank was about to say that Raymond had never been in or seen a real helicopter, but he stopped. One of the other kids said, "That's great that you know a lot about that. Maybe one of these days you could go with us to the local airport and tell us what you know. We sure don't know much, do we, Frank?"

5. _______ Aubrey has a condition in which she is very sensitive to sounds. Sometimes she will leave a group to go sit by herself in a quiet place. Lilly followed her and asked if Aubrey would tell her about it. Aubrey said she would tell her all about how it felt and what helped. Lilly sat down and said, "I'm a very good listener. Tell me about it."

Name____ Date______________

Worksheet 169

Treating Others with Patience

Allowing others some extra time to deal with a situation or come up with a response is one way to be a good citizen. The following situations are ones in which an individual might be trying your patience. How could you respond?

1.

I can do impressions of all kinds of people! Watch! Watch! Here is me doing the principal!

Mark, we just want to eat lunch.

2.

I have just about finished with this map. I know you're all in a hurry to get this project finished. I need a little more time to make it look really good. It looks like a mess right now.

Treating Others with Patience (continued)

3.
We are discussing things about our childhood in our psychology class, but I am very uncomfortable talking about my past. I don't really want to join in that conversation.
4.
I'm not very good at talking around people; I get so nervous. I know I need to give this little speech, but I would rather just read it than talk off the top of my head. Do you think I could use notes? I have 50 note cards. Oops, I just dropped them!
5.
I ... think ... I think that I ... would like to order a ... hamburger. Could I ... have ketchup ... and mustard ... with the hamburger? Maybe ... maybe I should get chicken ... chicken nuggets instead. I ... need to think about this .....

Name____ Date______________

Worksheet 170

Sharing Your Skills and Influence

What are these characters doing to help someone by using their own skills and influence?

1.

Everyone's coming to my house on Sunday to watch the Green Bay Packers game. Come and join us. You'll have to wear a green and gold sweatshirt though! That is, if you want to be part of the PACK.

2.

Some girls are so mean. Every once in a while I have to remind those particular "ladies" to cool it and watch what they say. My circle is not into bullying, ever.

Sharing Your Skills and Influence (continued)

3.

4.

Hey, Nance, that sweater is really cute, but I think you can do better. I happen to have some sweaters that I was going to give to my cousin who is about your size. Why don't we have a makeover day when you come over and we'll try on clothes?
Jack, if you get invited to Lauren's party, make sure you clean up and wear clean jeans. Lauren's mom is really particular about having everything real nice and everybody looking good. Lauren doesn't care, but we all know that her mom is a neat freak, so we try to make her happy. Sound good?

Sharing Your Skills and Influence (continued)

5.

Martha, I would really like to get to know you. Would you be interested in joining a yoga class with me on weekends? It's fun and very beginner-friendly.